KINGS OF LIT[illegible]E

EDITED BY

SIR A. T. QUILLER-COUCH

Under the Northern Lights

ALAN SULLIVAN

J. M. DENT & SONS LTD
LONDON

Made in Great Britain
at the
Aldine Press · Letchworth · Herts
for
J. M. DENT & SONS LTD
Aldine House · Bedford Street · London
First published in this edition 1928
Last reprinted 1969

SBN: 460 08163 2

CONTENTS

UNDER THE NORTHERN LIGHTS

TRADE

AJIDAMO, the Squirrel, pushed his way through the undergrowth. He had been walking thus, silently and observantly, for hours, while he made the round of his traps. Like a brown ghost he came, guided by a broken twig here, an overturned leaf there, and other signs so faint as to be imperceptible save to the eye of an aborigine. It was mid-afternoon when he reached a ridge where most of the rock was bare and the forest pushed up close on either side. Close to the ridge, in a clump of ground hemlock, was a stream on whose banks the snow still lay a few inches deep. Beside the stream glinted a small steel trap. In the trap was a mink with russet-brown fur.

Ajidamo grunted complacently, opened the spring, dropped his quarry into a sack, where it nestled softly against an otter and a stone marten, then took his way silently along the ridge. He did not hurry. The day was fine, and he was at home wherever sunset might overtake him.

Three hundred yards farther on lay a young Norway pine overthrown by winter winds. Its black roots lifted grotesquely into the air and carried patches of earth and moss. In one of these tangles Ajidamo noticed a piece of rock different from any he had ever seen. It was strongly gripped, as though in a man's hand, and the level rays of the sun seemed to pass through it. He looked at it curiously. To the ordinary observer it would have resembled a bit of semi-transparent alabaster enclosing a twist of gilded lace. To a mining man it would have been a sample of high-grade, free-milling gold ore. But to Ajidamo it was only something different. And just for that reason he knocked it free, examined it closely with unwinking black eyes, and dropped it in beside the stone marten.

He tramped on, slept that night five miles away, continued his silent pilgrimage another twenty miles, and reached his winter camp at sundown. Here he thawed out his take, pulled the precious skins inside out over the slim red bodies, threw the bodies into the pot, and stretched the fur over thin, wedge-shaped pieces of wood. He thought nothing more about the piece of rock, till presently the oldest grandchild, rummaging in the sack with reddened fingers, pulled the thing out. Ajidamo took it, held it questioningly toward his daughter, and, when she shook her head, tossed the fragment carelessly back.

Storms raged and ceased, snow fell and melted, the sun grew stronger, water began to run over the rocks, the wilderness seemed to yawn luxuriously in the growing warmth after months of rigid slumber, and presently spring came to the Northern wilderness. There was a slackening of the bones of earth, the whiteness of rabbit-fur became patched with dirty brown, from the skies drifted the calling of geese and swans on the long trek to the Arctic, while a thousand streams burst their manacles and went singing through the woods. It was at this time that Ajidamo gathered together his winter's catch. Then he lifted his canoe from the place where it had lain covered with spruce boughs since last November, sewed up its gaping seams with fine strips of tamarac root, sealed them with cloth dipped in hot resin, and went off to the nearest Hudson Bay post, which was a hundred miles away, as quietly as a dry leaf moves in front of a puff of wind.

• • • • •

The Hudson Bay factor is a taciturn man, clothed generally in nondescript garments and always with a great authority. His word goes forth as the law of the Northern wilderness, because it has never been broken. To Ojibway and Iroquois, to Yellowknife and Cree, to Piegan and Blackfoot, that word is the same. When it comes to a matter of trade, the bargain is hard and the terms are stiff, but the faith is absolute. So it happens that in a season of the year the hunters turn from the smoke of a thousand camp-fires and push their canoes over leagues of water, black and brown, by lake and rapid and cataract, to do business as their fathers did it, and with the offspring of those who traded with their fathers.

Thus came Ajidamo to the post on Crooked Lake.

He came at his own pace, a leisurely twenty miles a day, his eyes active on the journey, for when one lives by eye and ear and the strength of one's sinews, there is much to be learned be one ever so old, and Ajidamo was only seventy. He caught a few fish, mostly in the rapids, where pickerel were to be had for the taking, snared a few rabbits, drank a good deal of tea, and smoked incessantly. In the bottom of the canoe, tied neatly in the sack, were mink, otter, marten, a few fisher skins and one cross fox. He hoped for a good deal from the latter.

Nearing the post, he fell in with others on the same errand. Some he knew personally, such as Wa-wa, the Wild Goose, and Ah-tick, the Caribou, but they did not talk much, making camp the last night a little way apart on the river's bank, so that their fires blinked like a succession of the red eyes of animals that came down in the dark to drink when drinking could be done safely. Nor was there any hustling for bargains when the post was reached, it being common knowledge that prices did not vary. Each of them came up in turn, emptied his catch on the rough-hewn counter, and waited voicelessly till the factor had checked the number of skins and formed his own opinion of their condition and value. And while he waited, there was a swift, narrow-eyed scrutiny of the loaded shelves, bulging with all that the heart of man, woman or child could desire. Not the least thing to the credit of Ajidamo and his friends was the fact that no Hudson Bay post reported losses by theft.

When it came to Ajidamo's turn, he up-ended his sack, and with the fur there tumbled out that forgotten fragment of rock. It fell to the floor, lying unnoticed till the bargaining was done. Ajidamo owed fifty dollars from last year, and when this had been liquidated he still found himself able to get most of the things he wanted—cloth, a red shawl for his daughter, powder for recharging Winchester cartridges, lead, three new traps, a four-pound axe-head, a net with four-inch mesh for white-fish, a slab of salt pork, tea, sugar, baking-powder. These he collected, making a neat pile that rose beside him. The factor put in a pound of tobacco as a present, then leaned forward.

"What's yon bit of rock?"

Ajidamo gave it to him and shook his head. "I don't know. Maybe no good."

The factor twisted it between his hard fingers. "Where did it come from?"

Ajidamo made a gesture that took in the entire country lying north of Crooked Lake. "Up there. Long way. Me find him two months gone—I guess no good."

Followed a little silence. There were rumours of gold in the district, talks of gold around a good many camp-fires, and a trickle of prospectors from the area farther south. The factor had a month-old paper that came in by dog team the week before, and there was an article in that. He didn't take it very seriously. This was a good fur country, and that ought to be enough for him, and he didn't know anything about minerals. But one could never tell. He turned the thing round so that the light fell into it, and thought it very pretty.

"Want it?" he asked Ajidamo.

The old hunter shook his head. "Me think no good," he said, and gathered up his purchases.

. . . . .

Kelly was plainly out of luck. He lay on his back in his tent, slapped at mosquitoes and cursed creation in general. For a year now he had been scratching rock to no purpose. Other men had made good strikes, cleaned up a pile, and had either got out of the country or else done the same thing over again. But on the Abitibi River the Irish seemed to have lost their luck.

Added to this was the sobering fact that he was nearly broke. The small sum of forty dollars separated him from that bankruptcy which meant that he would have to work for someone else, a fate that all real prospectors dread. To get up in the morning and feel that you couldn't go where you wanted to go was something worse than death. It stared Kelly in the face now. If one adds to this the further truth that he was nearly out of grub, the venom of his language will be the more understandable.

He lighted a pitch-pine knot, took a torn map from his packsack and studied it intently. It was thumbed and mutilated beyond repair, but still decipherable. In the flicker, and between slaps at the mosquitoes, which were now worse than before, he saw that the post of Crooked Lake lay about two days' journey off. H B P, the map said, from which Kelly knew that there was to be obtained there all that made life feasible in the wilderness. He reckoned that the district was no good, never had been and never would be any good, but, because he was in the middle of it, decided to give it just one more chance. So at daybreak he started off, making a bee-line for Crooked Lake, and wondering what the Scotchman, who was bound to be in charge, would have the nerve to ask for a fifty-pound sack of self-rising flour. He arrived on the eve of the second day in a worse temper than ever. Mackintosh looked in his angry eye and waited placidly. He was a man of experience.

"'Twill be ten cents a pound, cash," he said easily.

Kelly gulped. "It's a hold-up—three cents a pound in Toronto."

"Ye're no forced to buy it if ye dinna want it," said Mackintosh.

"You know I've got to buy it, but it's a whale of a price."

"Maybe. I'm not disputin' that, but it didn't exactly fly here, ye ken."

"Can I have twenty dollars credit?"

Mackintosh shook his head. "If ye were an Indian; but I'll no trust a white man in this country." He paused a moment. "Happen ye're not a squaw man? That might help."

This left Kelly breathless, and he rocked with anger. "Think I'd marry an Indian?" he hissed.

"Ye might do a sight waur," said Mackintosh calmly. "I've married ane mysel'. D'ye want that flour?"

Kelly swallowed his wrath and bought. With the flour were other things, and while the factor sorted them out his visitor's eye fell on a fragment of rock that glinted whitely on a corner shelf.

"What's that?" he said, pointing.

"Naethin' but a bit that ane of ma customers left here last winter. D'ye ken what it is?"

Kelly fingered the thing, and his pulse began to pound. Never in his dreams had he seen a specimen like this. A thousand dollars to the ton if it was worth a cent.

"Careful," he whispered to himself, "careful now!" and laid it casually back on the counter.

"It might be worth following up. Where does the Indian live? I'll drop in if I'm in that direction."

"I'm no sure where he is the noo, but he wintered on Loon Lake. That's a hundred mile from here."

"What's he call himself?" Kelly's voice creaked a little.

• • • • •

Ajidamo sat in the sun, making a new cedar paddle which would be as light as a feather. One end of it was against his stomach, and he drew the knife toward him with long, smooth strokes, while the shavings fell away in neat, regular curls. Presently he saw a distant flicker on the glassy water. There was a white man coming.

Kelly floated up half an hour later, laid his own paddle across the thwarts, leaned forward and lit his pipe.

"*Boozhoo,*" he said.

"*Boozhoo,*" replied Ajidamo. "*Meno keejegud.*"

Kelly admitted that it was a fine day, took another look at the camp, and came ashore. He had given a good deal of thought to this interview. When one dealt with an Indian, the thing was not to be too earnest or impetuous. It made the other fellow suspicious. One led up to what one wanted, then touched on it casually in passing. So he, too, lay in the sun and talked generalities of the wilderness, while the paddle took shape under Ajidamo's firm brown fingers. It was not till evening that he got round to the subject.

"Much rock about here?"

The old man waved a hand at the purple horizon. "Plenty rock—some places." He knew what Kelly sought before the canoe touched shore, and Kelly knew that he knew. But that didn't alter anything.

"Much fur last winter?"

"Some," said Ajidamo, and put a kettle on the fire.

"Smoke?" Kelly tossed over a plug of tobacco.

The ancient aristocrat nodded, filled his pipe, and relapsed into silence. He wasn't interested, or even amused. He ripped up the belly of a five-pound pickerel, carved out its backbone with two swift strokes, and laid it in the pan. Kelly contributed a lump of salt pork. The meal was shared without speech. Kelly glanced at the grave, aquiline face and felt like choking, but it was no use trying to hustle a man for whom time and space and riches and the world in general did not exist. Still, there remained the outrageous fact that this relic of a vanishing race possessed knowledge that was worth a barrel of money. He decided to wait a little longer.

An hour before sunset he unrolled his blankets, and there fell out a piece of white quartz. He pitched it across to Ajidamo.

"Ever see any rock like that?"

Ajidamo fingered it, and knew at once all about it—the upturned Norway pine, earth and moss in its roots, and this glistening in the sun. So that was what had brought the stranger. He rather liked Kelly, because the latter hadn't jumped down his throat, bombarding him with questions. There was a way of doing everything—even talking about rocks.

"Over there," he said, pointing west. "Me see him last spring."

"Far?"

"Two days."

Kelly laid a hot coal in the bowl of his pipe just to make sure of his nerves. They were quite steady.

"How much-go there?"

Ajidamo considered this patiently. He usually asked two dollars and a half a day for what little work he had ever done, and he never got anything for the return trip, because one place was the same as another as far as he was concerned. But this time, and since something assured him that Kelly was very much in earnest, he decided to take a chance and double the charge.

"Ten dollars," he said.

Kelly shook his head. "Too much. Give you five."

. . . . .

Paterson had a combined office and residence, a wooden structure twelve by twenty-four, on the outskirts of the town of Porcupine. Over the door was a large sign: "Mines and Mining Shares Bought and Sold." He lived in the other end—twelve by twelve. In the office were shelves carrying samples of ore from various properties. The sight of them was apt to impress a client, and helped to keep up his enthusiasm, for he had never bought a share or sold a mine. His capital was five thousand dollars.

He was lounging about in front when Kelly came up the road, staggering under a packsack which, though it was only half filled, seemed extremely heavy. He dropped it opposite the office for a rest, and Paterson caught the grinding creak of broken rock. He strolled over and offered the stranger a cigarette.

"Got anything?"

Kelly glanced at the broad, red, good-natured face and rather liked it.

"I've got the original horned mint," he said. "What have you got?"

"A few thousand dollars. What's your hurry?"

Kelly brightened, then hesitated. "What do you call a few?"

"Enough to buy the real thing when I see it."

Kelly went in. Paterson talked about mines in general and it was some time before they got round to the packsack. Neither wanted to seem in a hurry, and Paterson played the same rôle as Kelly when the latter did diplomatic work in the camp of Ajidamo. The scale of intelligence ascended.

The up-ended packsack disgorged its burden. Gold, and lots of it—gold in little filaments and plates and grains, frozen, seemingly, in the milky quartz. Paterson had seen nothing like this before.

"Not so bad," he said evenly. "Where is it?"

Kelly laughed at him. "Nothing doing, pilgrim. I'm no free information bureau."

Paterson passed on undisturbed. He didn't expect to be told yet, but it was worth trying.

"Much of it?"

That was horse sense, and Kelly loosened up.

"She's about eight hundred feet long and seven wide. I stripped her in seven places—all about the same. Some of it's richer than this, and some not so g od. Can you beat it?"

Paterson had a lump in his throat. "Far from the water?"

"About a quarter-mile."

"Hard to get at?"

"Easy as breathing."

"Cut loose, stranger. What's your name and your price?"

Kelly leaned back luxuriously. He had been thinking about the price ever since Ajidamo led him up to the overturned Norway pine, and he actually saw the thing he had dreamed of for years. The figure had varied a good deal on the way out, but never got any smaller. In the glow of the present moment he decided to take a chance and double it.

"I want ten thousand down, twenty in three months, and another twenty in six."

"Give you half that, and it's a deal," said Paterson.

. . . . .

James Randolph, of New York, sat at a corner table in the dining-room of the Porcupine Hotel. He was a quiet man, very silent, and had a keen grey eye. There was nothing conspicuous about Randolph, nothing to betray the fact that he was a noted geologist; nothing to suggest that he represented enough money to buy the entire township and all in it twice over. He ate slowly and without interest, glancing occasionally at the very mixed assemblage. It was nothing unusual to him.

Two strangers came in and annexed the adjoining table, one large, red-faced, and of the type recognisable as "mining broker," the other evidently just out of the woods. They were not drunk, but very cheerful, and Randolph wondered where they got it. One ate peas with his knife, very neatly and without spilling any, while the other, apparently not hungry, ranged a row of quartz specimens in front of his plate. Randolph noted these, and forgot about their owner. Ten minutes later he strolled out, took a chair on the verandah near the dining-room door, and began to smoke thoughtfully.

"Eight hundred long, seven wide, and pans heavy all the way. She's the original nickel-plated mint, pilgrim, and you ought to be tickled down the back." The words came quite clearly.

Presently the large man appeared and struck off down the road. Randolph pitched away his cigarette and paced slowly in that direction.

At two o'clock Paterson had the thing pretty well thought out. He proposed to make his pile out of this one deal, as it was not likely anything of the same sort would come his way again. He had to find another twenty thousand in six months, so a fair price would be a hundred thousand in five. He was gloating over the samples when a stranger chanced in and asked the way to the Lockmaster Mine.

The latter got the information and was about to walk on, when he glanced casually at the specimens on Paterson's table.

"That looks to be pretty good stuff."

Paterson surmised that it was, the best stuff that ever came out of the darned district, and, what's more, he owned it.

"Whereabouts?" asked the stranger.

Paterson grinned. "That exact information comes after a deal and not before it."

"Far from here?"

"No—easy as breathing?"

"You in the mining business?"

"In a sort of way. Friends of mine might put some money in. But I'm told there's been a lot lost up here."

Paterson chuckled. "'Tain't lost if you know where it is."

Randolph didn't answer. He was wondering how much the other man knew about mines and mining.

"Is this much of a vein you've got?"

The figures came out, and he looked up rather wistfully.

"It's this way with me. I'm free to buy something for my friends to develop. That stuff seems to have gold in it, and in a general way I'm ready for a gamble. What's your price?"

Paterson told him, but he shook his head.

"Figure's too big for me. Doesn't matter. I'm going on to the silver country to-morrow, and just came over here for a look. I've real money to spend, but not as much as that. Must keep something for development." He got up, smiling.

Paterson reflected. He'd rather like to say he'd bought a lode and sold it in four hours. And perhaps the late vendor was a bit of a liar. "Suppose you made an offer?"

"My limit is just half your price, and you'd have to show me the lode before you got the cheque."

"Just as the other fellow has to show me before he gets his, eh?"

"Exactly."

"Shake on it," said Paterson.

• • • • •

Ajidamo had heard it all afternoon, a low, constant rumble that sounded like distant thunder, but was always in the same place. It grew louder as he paddled, till, rounding the point, he saw ahead a great gash in the wooded slope of the land. It was now something more than eighteen months since he had been here last, and then he came to show a stranger the spot where a young Norway pine lay with its roots in the air.

He stopped paddling a quarter-mile from shore, and drifted motionless while comprehension slowly deepened in his dark eyes. Up the hill, and just at the spot he remembered, was a tall timber thing on top of which was a wheel that went round very fast. Below this descended a nest of great buildings. On one side houses, the only kind of house he had ever seen, with a white road running between them. There were a dock, two or three launches, scows, men sprinkled everywhere, long piles of wood, and always that queer rumble. Close to the water he saw a log shanty he took to be the store. At that he dipped his paddle, and the canoe moved as does a thought in the mind of a lazy man.

He got out on a strip of sand that wasn't there before. Sharp and very white, it was being carried down by a trough from the lowest and biggest building of all. He had never seen sand like that before. Ajidamo could not know that the ore from which it was crushed had lain three hundred feet below the roots of the Norway pine. He could not know that the Broadvenue Mine—thus christened because its owners did business in a marble-lined eyrie near the corner of the two most famous streets of a very famous city—had repaid half its purchase price in the first month's run. He could not know what happened to Kelly, or Paterson, or any of them, nor would he have cared. What he did know was that his share of all this was five dollars. And at that he grunted softly.

The storekeeper at the Broadvenue was not versed in the ways of the country, also he knew nothing and cared nothing about Indians. So when Ajidamo came in on moccasined feet and, unwrapping four silver dollars from a bit of caribou skin, asked for flour, he got much less than he should have had. This time the price was doubled, not halved. Nor was he given a plug of tobacco, which was gross discourtesy as well as a tactical error, and in general he received such treatment as no Hudson Bay factor would have dreamed of extending to a member of the most ancient family of the land.

"Is that all you want?"

"Yes," said Ajidamo.

"Then clear out, and take this. Don't eat it—it's to wash with. You need it."

Ajidamo looked at him, but did not touch the soap. The young man, knowing Third Avenue, thought he knew everything, but did not understand that look. There was dignity in it, and a silent pride born of thousands of years of freedom, and a sort of vague wonder. The aged hunter had become used to something different, and a certain mutual civility, and prices that, if hard, were at least stable. So he felt that this change, and these bad manners, and the rumble that shook the earth, and this short measure, were in a way all his own fault. Furthermore, everyone seemed to be doing well in this matter except himself. He picked up the flour and went slowly out.

Halting on the white sand, he took a piece of quartz from his pocket. It was about the same size as the first one, but infinitely richer, and nearly half gold. He had found it three months previously in a spot only a day's journey distant, but in such a corner that it was very unlikely to be found again. The last piece had earned five dollars, and he had hoped that this one would bring him as much. Perhaps it was worth ten.

He turned it over in his smooth, callous palm for a moment, then pitched it into the lake.

THE EYES OF SEBASTIEN

THIS is a tale of the big timber that grows in league-long patches where the headwaters of the Saguenay find their birth amongst tumbled foothills of the Laurentian range. Thence flows the Saguenay, a chill and formidable stream, gathering volume as it moves southward with countless tributaries from unknown lakes and moose-trampled marshes, loitering on its way through stretches of cedar-bordered solitude, flinging itself headlong over cataracts where the tawny water rages thunderously day and night, ever more deep, forbidding and austere, till at last it merges majestically with the great St. Lawrence, the mother of many rivers, and spends itself between the thousand-foot crags of Capes Trinity and Eternity.

All along the Saguenay it is a French country, as French as when two hundred years ago the peasants of Brittany and Normandy first fared northward into the unexplored wilderness. Amid the big timber and beside unnamed waters they raised their log-hewn walls, with the mud-chinked joints, the tiny deep-set windows and the massive roofs that must bear the weight of winter snows. Out of the forest they carved their farms, planting grain between the unconquerable roots, drawing sustenance from wood and stream, beating off marauding Indians, gathering in the long winter evenings round pine-heaped hearths, utterly alone save when in summer the yellow bows of a canoe glided round a point, and a missionary Jesuit Father landed from Quebec; or when in winter the man of God tramped, solitary, through endless miles of big timber on his errand of mercy and peace.

But always there was talk of France, with lingering, poignant pictures of the land they had left, of the red roofs of Quiberon that look across the bay at Croise and the cobbled streets of Rennes that lead to the swift waters of the Vilaine.

In one of the patches of timber on Lac St. Luc there is a lumber-camp, a nest of long buildings, ten feet high, that occupy a roughly cleared space close to the water's edge. From the camp there radiates a maze of winter roads traversed by a hundred lumberjacks in gaudy woollen capotes, with axes and saws over their shoulders, and down these roads, which all slope gently to the lake, great logs are drawn, to be dumped, rumbling, on the ice. All through the day one can hear, near and far, the crash of big timber toppling earthward, the creak of straining harness, the crack of whips, the stroke of axes and the whine of distant saws. At night there is talk beside great cast-iron stoves stuffed with fuel, much smoke, the drone of winter winds and the plaintive hoot of the great white owl.

It fell on a day when the sun shone bright and the snow was like a sparkling blanket, that a man emerged from the Saguenay trail and struck across Lac St. Luc. He walked with a long, easy swing, bending a little forward beneath the weight of his pack. Threading his way between the piles of logs, he halted at the door of the main building, twisted his feet free of snowshoes and entered.

"Hallo!" he said with a smile. "I have again arrived."

The cook looked round, and straightway forgot his cooking, for the new-comer was none other than Antoine Carnot the peddler—the bringer of news—the teller of tales—the confidential go-between in the wilderness—the human link with the outside world. Antoine was all of these, and more. A bit of a doctor, a bit more of a lawyer, a shrewd trader, and withal possessed of unfailing humour and a heart of gold. No wonder that Pierre Colange forgot his cooking and hurried forward, hands outstretched.

"Ten thousand welcomes, *mon vieux*. No, you shall not talk till you have eaten. Behold, a partridge which was for the boss, but eat and say nothing. The wind makes a chill in the stomach, but you have an hour before the men come in. Fill thyself, and say nothing till afterwards."

Antoine nodded and obeyed, while Pierre watched him admiringly. Then there was news, much news from a dozen villages, while the pack was unrolled and its contents spread on a table in the corner. Knives and neckties, shirts and razors and mouth-organs, jimcracks and cheap jewellery, studs and celluloid collars—the result of Antoine's annual trip to Quebec. A great man was Antoine; had he not once sent a telegram to Montreal and got an anwser the very next day, and he right there in Quebec all the time! Presently his wares were displayed to his satisfaction, and he sent Pierre a swift glance.

"Jean Deslormes, he is still here?"

Pierre nodded. "He makes good money, forty dollars a month—and spends nothing save for tobacco."

"I was at Villeneuve this day two weeks ago," said Antoine thoughtfully, "and saw the girl Marie Fisette. They are betrothed."

Pierre laughed at this. "Does not the whole camp know it, and how many times has Jean not told us! Every morning he goes along the road making verses to that girl with his mouth. It is well that he cannot write—but perhaps I do not understand such things. I made no verses to my Henriette."

Antoine looked a little grave. "Sebastien was also at Villeneuve, and full of anger when he heard of the betrothal. Marie told me that he said strange and threatening things, that she should never marry Jean. Then he barked something like a wolf, and she did not see him again."

"Loup Garou!" whispered Pierre under his breath.

It was a word of awe through the outlying French country. The story of the Loup Garou, that strange and malign combination of man and wolf, had come across with them from the hills of Brittany. The belief still held north of the Laurentians. It was always an old dog wolf, tenanted by some evil and human spirit, endowed with wild powers of murder and revenge, a lean grey beast that patrolled the winter hills and sent his savage note drifting down into solitary villages where simple folk gathered closer round the fire and glanced apprehensively at the window-fastenings. Sometimes it was a man who took the form of a wolf to serve his dread purpose, and became again human when his deadly part was played.

This had been whispered of Sebastien behind his back. Where the man came from none knew, only that calamity came with him. He was small, dark and very active, with hollow cheeks and burning eyes, and moved about through the French country, seldom doing any work, but living apparently without effort. He was disliked and feared, but the folk made no protest—at least to Sebastien. There was the case of Georges Famieux who threw Sebastien out of his barn one evening, and next morning found his prize cow with her throat torn. One remembered that sort of thing in a district where cows were scarce. So now the good Antoine pushed out his lips and nodded gravely.

"Yes," he said thoughtfully, "it can be nothing else."

A little silence fell in the cook's camp, and both men had a vision of Marie Fisette of the parish of Villeneuve, Marie the prettiest girl north of Cape Trinity, with her flaxen hair and white skin like milk and a smile that was remembered and treasured enviously in every lumber-camp on the Saguenay. They said that she chose Jean Deslormes when she saw him driving logs through the chute at Les Arables. And what Jean did then ought to be enough for any girl.

"They will be married this summer—yes?" asked Pierre.

And just at this moment the door opened without sound, and Sebastien himself strolled in. He rubbed his long hands to set the blood going, glanced shrewdly at the two men and stared meaningly toward the heaped platters on the stove. Pierre gave him food, this being the law of the wilderness, while Antoine began to re-arrange his stock. Both were a little breathless. Presently Sebastien pushed away his plate.

"Without doubt, Pierre, you are the best cook in the Saguenay camps. I will tell them so in Villeneuve." He lit his pipe and began to smoke contentedly.

"You go then to Villeneuve?" hazarded Antoine.

"Yes, I start at once, this very day."

"By the Saguenay trail?"

Sebastien sent him an inscrutable smile. "My trail is my own, Antoine"; then, meaningly, "let him follow who can."

"It is ninety miles to Villeneuve as the goose flies. What takes you there in midwinter?"

"The thing that takes all men to all places no matter what the season. The face of a woman."

Pierre lifted a kettle from the stove, and the

lid rattled. "Is it then that Sebastien marries at his age?"

"What is age to the man who desires? In five days I shall have what has been desired by many."

He announced this in a voice that lifted as he spoke, and surveyed the others with burning, insolent eyes as though daring them to protest. There was in his manner something suggesting that he had at his disposal powers of which they knew nothing. He leaned a little forward, every line of his sinewy body resembling an animal crouched to spring, and there was but one animal in the minds of the others. He was known to travel swiftly, and always alone, but no man had ever found his tracks. And though he could not marry till after he had been in Villeneuve for at least three days, he now stated he would marry in five. That left two days to cover ninety miles, measured as the goose flies. There was but one beast in the big timber that could travel like this. Antoine glanced furtively at Pierre, and the latter gave the faintest nod. "Loup Garou," their lips signalled.

Sebastien got up, stretched himself, gave a short laugh and strode to the door. "For a good dinner, *bien merci, mon vieux*. It is I who shall feed you when the logs come down past Villeneuve in the spring. Every woman of the family of Fisette is an incomparable cook. We shall be ready, Marie and I."

For a moment after he disappeared there was silence in the camp, till both men stepped quickly to the window. Sebastien had reached the ice, and putting on his snowshoes already struck southward across Lac St. Luc. He walked swiftly, dwindling as they watched to a dark speck that vanished round a nearby point. Then Antoine looked at his friend and swore a great oath.

"Jean—where is Jean?"

"He comes with the sawyers in ten minutes. But wait, I will call them now."

Pierre went out and smote with a poker on a large steel triangle that hung close to the door. Straightway the woods throbbed with a clear singing note that lifted through the green tops and caused a dropping of axes and cessation of droning saws, till down the winter roads trooped the lumberjacks, hungry as bears and chanting musically of Alluette and La Claire Fontaine. At their head came Jean Deslormes, a young, tawny-haired giant, straight as a hemlock and shouldered like a bull moose. He caught sight of Antoine outside the camp, and, running forward, flung round him a pair of gigantic arms.

"Ah, c'est le vieux Papa Carnot. When didst thou arrive, and hast thou perchance been at a place called Villeneuve?"

Antoine struggled for breath. "I would first that some young fools learn their strength—and use it less," he gasped—then, in a whisper, "No, I have not visited Villeneuve since a fortnight past, but——"

"A fortnight! That is but a moment, while I have not been there for two months. Is there nothing then to tell me, no message?"

"Shout not thy love to the whole camp, my son. There was one here a moment ago who even now is on his way to Villeneuve."

"Have you then sold all your stock to the good Pierre, and send out for more?"

Antoine shook his head. "The name of the traveller is Sebastien, and he goes fast."

"Le Loup Garou," said Jean grimly. "But why to Villeneuve?"

"In search of one Marie Fisette, who he swears will be his in the space of five days. My son will need all his strength, and must act very quickly. Let go, Jean, you break my arm!"

"He took what trail?—quick!" Jean swayed a little, with such a tremor as runs through the brown column of a pine when the saw eats at its heart.

"He said that his trail was his own, and that any might follow who could, then struck south around the point. Shut up thy Marie in thy breast, my son, and hasten; but"—and here Antoine sent him an eloquent glance—"search not always for the form of a man as you travel."

Jean hurled himself into the sleeping-camp.

In ten minutes he was out on the ice, and, clearing the strewn logs, swung forward toward the first southerly point of Lac St. Luc. Thus led Sebastien's trail—long, narrow tracks with the points of the shoes turned up a little more than was usual in a bush country and the tail of one with an outward twist. He would remember that. They took him round that point, straight as an arrow-flight past the next one and on to a glassy patch where the water had come up and turned a mile of Lac St. Luc into a looking-glass. Here he slipped off his shoes, trotted across and cast about close to the shore line. There was no more trail.

He stood for a moment, shaking his head like a great puzzled dog. This was the trail that any might follow who could! His lips became dry as he doubled back, and, picking up his own tracks, traversed the edge of the patch till he came to them again. "By Gar!" he whispered. "By Gar!"

Eighty miles due south was Villeneuve, with Marie and tinkling sleigh-bells and pearl-grey smoke climbing from heaped roofs. Somewhere to the south was something nosing swiftly through the big timber. "Search not always for the form of a man," Antoine had said. Jean jerked out a tense petition to St. Joseph, patron and guardian of the family Fisette, then put on his shoes.

There was moonlight by seven. It turned the snow to a pale purple, on which blue-black shadows of big timber lay in wide and parallel bars. He tramped across these, bar to bar, leaning forward with massive arms swinging, his legs working like pistons; a vast engine of a man moving in a white flurry and spouting deep-drawn jets of vapour. There was no sound save the creak of shoes, and a muffled thud as some overburdened cedar doffed its load of snow and straightened its tender branches in the stinging air. Presently he came to a frozen swamp. On the other side of this, where the shadows began again, stood a lone wolf.

It vanished as he stared, merging like one shadow into another. Jean paused for a moment while a new thought dawned, and struck off sharp to the right. Two hundred yards away he found it—a wolf track—the triangular pad with the long sharp projecting toe and narrow trailing heel. He followed this back a quarter-mile, noting that it paralleled his own, curving where his curved and holding south for Villeneuve. And then Jean knew.

At four in the morning the moon went down in a bank of cloud. Came a whine of wind and a few drifting flakes. The woods grew dark. By this time Jean was very hungry, and therefore felt cold, for in these latitudes the body, like a boiler, demands fuel. He shoveled aside the snow, made fire and tea, searching the gloom with quick and furtive glances, crossing himself between gulps. In ten minutes he heard a rabbit squeal. That meant death in the ground hemlock near by. Something else was feeding there, and resting—resting.

As the goose flies it is ninety miles from the camp on St. Luc to Villeneuve, but as man travels not less than a hundred. As a wolf might go it is perhaps ninety-five. At sunrise Jean knew it was the same this time for man and wolf. There was not so much concealment now. He saw the gaunt, grey form flitting, wraith-like, between brown trunks, a malign beast with deep, lean shoulders and bony, arrow-shaped head. It rested when he rested, ate when he ate—and kept always a little in advance. By mid-afternoon it became difficult to think of anything else and he grew very sleepy. It was only the vision of Marie with her flaxen hair, her smiling mouth and white arms that held him awake. At sundown he knew that he must sleep if only for half an hour, or he would lose his way. There were no stars this time, and no moon. He made two fires of green birch-logs, laid spruce-boughs between them, pulled the hood of his capote over his nose and stretched out.

Instantly, it seemed he began to dream. There was no loup garou now, but only love and the whiteness of his girl's shoulder. At this unction his body yielded, his great muscles relaxed; till, smiling, he plunged into an abyss of slumber, lulled by tiny, crepitant voices from the surrounding forest. Then, horribly, the dream became distorted. Marie's face, so close to his own, changed to a grinning mask with black lifted lips, flat, sleek skull and malevolent yellow eyes. The yellow gave place to black. They were the eyes of Sebastien. Simultaneously came a strange warmth on his cheeks. He blinked. Something was staring at him, something so near that it shut out the rest of the world. He gave a cry and sprang to his feet. There was a scramble in the snow by the spruce-boughs. Jean Deslormes was alone again.

"Que le bon Dieu nous sauvasit!" he whispered, trembling.

From a southward ridge came answer, not by le bon Dieu, but the wild and haunting voice of the grey wolf. Through the big timber it drifted, savage, remote, but inescapable, the note of terror that in a season of the year carries its own message to fur and hide on the foothills of the Laurentians. To Jean it also carried a message, and he flung himself forward. It could not now be more than thirty miles to Villeneuve. He swung on, summoning his vast reserve of strength, plunging through underbrush where once he would have gone round, himself now a thing of the woods in the manner of his going—this giant with the mind of a child. He stayed not to rest or eat; he looked not again for the grey shape. Then a remembered hilltop—a winter road for drawing wood—an outlying pasture—the bark of a distant dog—and below, in the valley, revealed in the half-light of dawn, the spire of a church and the forty farms they called Villeneuve. Into the crisping air climbed forty pencils of pearl smoke, like the exhalations of those who slumbered yet a while ere facing the rigour of the day.

Jean tore downhill to the house of Marthe Fisette, the mother of Marie. It seemed that all was safe here. He paused at the door, heard inside the crackling of a fire, and knocked. At sight of him the old woman dropped an armful of wood.

"Jean!" she stammered, "how came you here?"

"As flies the goose from Lac St. Luc," he said, breathing hard; "and Marie?"

Marthe did not answer that, but stared at him wonderingly and with a touch of awe. "It is undoubtedly the good God who has sent you, but how did you know?"

"Antoine Carnot told me; and, hearing it, I waited for nothing——" He broke off, staring back. "Then it is true?"

"Sebastien?" Her lips framed the name.

He nodded. "Le Loup Garou! Together we have come from the camp on Lac St. Luc, and this morning he also is in Villeneuve, but in what form I know not. Last night when for a moment I closed my eyes he came and crouched beside me, breathing in my face, and would have torn my throat had I not suddenly awakened. I brought no gun, for one cannot kill a loup garou except with a bullet that has been blessed, and there was no priest on Lac St. Luc."

Marthe crossed herself fervently. "That is true—always it has been so."

"And the friends here—what do they say?"

"They shrug their shoulders—and say nothing. It is not well to quarrel with Sebastien. There is that affair of the good Famieux—a thing all remember."

"And Marie?" he demanded.

Marthe sent him a wintry smile. "Look over your shoulder, my son."

She was halfway down the ladder-stair from the room above; Marie with thick, yellow, knitted strands down her back, great, slumbrous roses in her smooth cheeks and drowsy love in her blue eyes. Jean gave a huge, gusty sigh of delight, put out his mighty arms and lifted her as one picks up an acorn. She hid her face in his capote.

"My little one," he said softly, "my little partridge; thou art safe here, very safe."

Presently they put food before him, and he ate ravenously, telling in snatches of the trip from Lac St. Luc—"ninety-five miles in forty-two hours, by Gar!"—while Marie clucked over him as though she were indeed a hen partridge, and Marthe busied herself without words between stove and table. Then Jean got up.

"I go now to Père Leduc, for we shall be married in three days. Also there is the matter of blessing some bullets." He paused, and waved a hand at the encircling bush. "It is there I shall use them."

"I also shall go," said Marie, divided between love and fear.

He shook his great head. "Such talk is not for my little bird, but thou shalt go so far as the store, and wait there. In three days my soul shall go everywhere with me. Be content, my swallow."

They went off down the packed road, where the snowplough had left four-foot ridges on either side, down to the store which was diagonally opposite the church and the house of the good Father. Here Jean left her clasped to the expansive bosom of Madame Famieux, crossed the road, kicked his shoepacks clean and found Père Leduc in his book-lined study. And books were precious north of the Laurentians. He spoke first of his heart's desire.

The Father nodded, smiling. He loved this young Anak, this son of the wilderness, with his great thews and child-like heart. Wise and tender was Père Leduc, a pure flame that glowed constantly, healing both minds and souls with a wide spiritual paternity.

"It is well for you both—and the good Marthe agrees?"

Jean nodded.

"Then I will call your names at vespers this very night, so that it may take place in three days. A good girl, your Marie. You go yourself back to Lac St. Luc?"

No, Jean would not do that. He had saved eight hundred dollars for a farm—and the farm of Georges Laurier was it not in the market? He paused a moment.

"There is another matter, *mon père*—that of these bullets." He held out a dozen, cupped in a gigantic palm. "May it please you to bless them?"

Père Leduc shook his head gently. Had he not been very wise he would have laughed. He knew—knew all about it. Individually he knew more than the entire village put together. Part of his strength was that he only revealed a fraction of his knowledge. And now he wanted to hear what this enormous child had to say—all of it.

"Tell me, my son."

Jean told him, from the very start, touching not on the physical marvel of the trip—for to Jean it was no marvel—but only on its terror. How did Sebastien leave the flooded patch on Lac St. Luc? What became of his shoes when he turned into a wolf? What did he mean by breathing in Jean's face? Why did he lead the way to Villeneuve? And most of all, what was the import of his boast about Marie? There must be an end to this—the end brought by a bullet that had been blessed. All Villeneuve was waiting for that.

Père Leduc put his hand on the young giant's shoulder, and spoke of tradition and legends and the powers of evil. "No, my son, you yourself are about to give answer to Sebastien—a final answer. You and this dear daughter of the parish will have my blessing, and not these bullets. When in three days you leave the church with Marie on your arm and joy in your heart you will have replied to Sebastien. He will have written himself down as a loud-speaking fool at whom not only the village of Villeneuve will laugh. That laugh will run up and down the Saguenay, till he will wish to walk into the stream itself to escape it. As for what you saw and searched for, but did not find on your way here, when the mind of a man be distraught with weariness, and perhaps fear, there is not much of which he can be very sure. You have had an evil dream, but it is past. Go now, my son, and take peace and happiness with you. Le bon Dieu is not forgetful of His children on the Saguenay."

Jean went out, cheered but not convinced. It was all very well to talk like that. But he *knew*, while the good Father had not been on the trail from St. Luc. He rubbed the bullets together in his pocket, stalked across to the store and gathered in Marie.

"Behold my wife in three days—this little spruce partridge," he said to the fat Madame Famieux. "*Viens donc, chérie*; there is much to talk of."

Up the shining road, arms linked, they walked,

while Jean told her the words of Père Leduc. Nor was Marie convinced. The good Father had never felt Sebastien's burning eyes, nor could he understand what it meant to a girl to shrink and quiver beneath that insolent stare till she became weak and helpless like a bird in a net.

"It is but one thing we shall do, Jean."

"What is that, my dove?"

"You shall meet Sebastien and take his promise, or make it, that there is an end to all this."

"Of what value then is the word of a wolf, could he speak it?" grunted Jean. Then, looking up, his heart leaped. Sebastien had rounded a bend in the road and came straight toward them. Marie saw him, shivered and clung the closer.

"Jean," she whispered, "not now!"

Drawing nearer he walked more slowly, staring first at the giant with strange, inscrutable gaze, then at Marie with a wild, unhuman hunger. His cheeks were hollow, but he moved lightly on his feet. They were not the feet of a man who had travelled ninety miles in forty-two hours—or less. He came level with them. Marie found herself pushed gently forward and past him. Jean stood motionless, every sinew in him turned to fire.

"Loup Garou," he said thickly, "Loup Garou, what seek you now?"

Sebastien did not speak, but lowered his lids, and from hot, half-veiled eyes sent the big man a look of contemptuous pity. So keen was it, so utterly penetrating, that Jean felt as though a hand were fumbling in his breast and groping for secrets. Then, as Sebastien was about to pass on, a mighty arm shot out and took him by the throat. He was shaken as a wolverine shakes a rabbit, shaken till his teeth chattered and flung headlong into the crusted snow. Jean turned on his heel and followed Marie.

"It is done, my turtle—and the wolf did not bark."

Late that night, after Jean had gone to sleep at the farm of Christophe Famieux, Marie talked long with her mother and told her the words of Père Leduc. Marthe could make no answer to these words, but found them nevertheless devoid of comfort. Presently she climbed the stair ladder, returning with a small image of St. Joseph, patron saint to every good Fisette.

"It is lead," she murmured, "and from Ste. Anne de Beaupré it came, where it was blessed by his Eminence from Quebec. Is it not that the head of the holy man is of the size of a bullet?"

Marie nodded, her eyes brightening.

"Then the rest of it I leave to thee, my pigeon. When thy mountain of a husband shall take thee from me in a sleigh to Beaulieu on the third day from this, see that the short gun of Christophe be thus loaded, and near at hand under the robes. It is in my mind that there will be need of that gun."

So on the third day, Gaston Roubidoux, sacristan, sent a rocking peal from the wooden church, and those of Villeneuve came in box-like sleighs stuffed with straw, and drawn by short-legged, round-bodied Percheron horses, to see the union of Jean and Marie —doubly intriguing because it spelled the humiliation of Le Loup Garou. Marie was all in white, with everlastings in her hair; Jean in a new, tight and very bright blue suit into which he just wedged his great body, celluloid collar anchored by a large rolled-gold stud, yellow tie and patent-leather shoes that hurt abominably. Then Père Leduc spoke words of peace and love, after which they all went to the house of Christophe, the largest in the village, where was given the marriage feast, with riotous quadrilles and great good feeling. And Sebastien had not been seen by anyone since three days—which added not a little to the general hilarity.

Beaulieu lay thirty miles away—or was it only three? Jean, being dizzy with happiness and pride, was not quite sure when at sunset he tucked his girl into the sleigh, wrapping the robes closely round her feet. There was plenty of straw underneath. Marthe had seen to that. The horses, pet team of Christophe, arching their glossy necks, dashed off with a jangle of bells amid laughter and cheers. The good Father nodded contentedly and turned homeward. These children of his—how gay and handsome they were!

Halfway to Beaulieu—the horses going like playful kittens—Marie pressing to his side—frosty roses in her cheeks—the blue eyes like stars—with all this Jean could hardly believe his own good fortune. What a noble day it had been, and how many others, even more wonderful, lay ahead! His feet were now very sore—that being from the dancing—his collar-stud was boring a hole in his gullet, but he was bursting with joy.

"My love," he breathed, "my soul—my little ptarmigan!"

Just at this moment there came from a belt of cedar hard by the pulsing howl of a timber wolf. Marie heard and shivered. Jean heard, and his heart stopped, then began to race. The Percherons heard, whinnied their alarm and plunged forward. Jean, gripping the reins, lashed out till the woods streamed past in a blur. If the road only held open he could make Beaulieu in an hour.

They swung into a clearing where the wind had got at the snow and the road was drifted level. Knee-deep toiled the Percherons, heads down, backs rippled with straining muscles. Jean stood up. Something shot across just ahead, turned, doubled back and made a ripping, darting stroke at the throat of the nearest horse.

"Quick, Jean, under the straw at my feet—the gun of Christophe with the head of St. Joseph!" panted Marie.

He wondered what St. Joseph had to do with it, but a gun was a gun, and, burrowing swiftly, he recognised the short, single-barrelled muzzle-loader with half-inch bore. Pushing the reins into the girl's hands, he cuddled his cheek against the brown stock—and waited. The near Percheron was bleeding at the throat. Again that lean, darting form, ears flattened back on the sleek skull, again the curving attack rapid as light.

The wolf was in mid-air when the foresight covered a grey shoulder for a fraction of time. Jean crooked his finger—saw horses rearing in a tangle of harness—heard Marie cry out in a jangle of bells. Then a lank, hairy body seemed to have been thrust away, and stretched, twitching, just ahead of the driving hoofs.

He snatched back the reins, forced on the Percherons and fetched them up, quivering, on top of the thing on the road. Here for a deadly second the steel-shod, dancing feet hammered down—down, till what lay beneath was a shapeless lump of bloody hide. Marie covered her eyes, but Jean, soothing his team, stared at it hard before he bent over and kissed the roses back to her cheeks. It was in his mind that the eyes of this wolf, instead of being long and yellow, had been large and dark and burning. They did not burn now. But he said nothing of this.

"My little weasel spoke of the gun of Christophe with the head of the good St. Joseph," he smiled. "And what did she mean by that?"

Marie told him, and for months after that there was little talk of Sebastien. Then summer arrived. The logs from St. Luc began to come down the Saguenay, and Jean was persuaded to help the drive through the chute of Les Arables. Marie went with him, and so it happened that Pierre Colange on a certain day did indeed sit at the table of an incomparable cook. The shanty that Jean knocked together stood close to the river, and the table was outside. They were talking of Sebastien when Pierre got up, shaded his eyes and stared hard at the tawny water.

"It has been in my mind, *mon vieux*, that we should meet him yet once again. What is that between the two hemlocks?"

He had come down with the logs—come from the unknown—and circled slowly in a great eddy. The smooth face was still unscarred. One sodden arm rested slack on the ribbed bark. The eddy brought him toward shore, bobbing as though something were twitching at his heels. The three gazed at each other, till Jean, remembering the prophecy of Père Leduc, lifted his brows and signalled.

"Go inside a moment, my little beaver. It is not for thee to see."

There is a cross underneath a jack-pine just below that eddy. Jean hewed it. On a flat stone at the foot is a small leaden image without a head. That was the thought of Marie. On the cross Pierre Colange, with some misgivings, put the name—one word. He could not decide what else, under the circumstances, one might safely say. It stood there after the drive went on and the following sweep had cleared every stranded log. Squirrels perched on it, rabbits hopped about it, red-headed woodpeckers sometimes tried their strength on its tough fibre. But nothing happened till Antoine Carnot passed in the autumn.

He saw it, read the one word and exactly appreciated the difficulty. So, smiling, he lit his pipe, squatted close, and began to carve with firm, deep strokes.

"Sebastien. Le Loup Garou," read the next lumberjack who came that way.

THE SPIRIT OF THE NORTH

I

Along the broad back of a great ridge the outline of a man moved slowly, tramping down the snow with wide-webbed shoes, whose symmetrical furrow stretched for leagues behind him. He leant forward as he walked, a tall figure muffled in a woollen tunic, the capote down over his hard blue eyes. The visible portion of his face was tanned a deep brown, his moustache a cake of ice, and the breath from his hot lungs spouted little jets of vapour into the tingling air.

All around the land was white, save where a scanty growth lined the gullies with thickets of spruce and birch. Over it sighed the winds of the North, whose chilling touch crept down from the Arctic circle and laid a crystallised finger of silence on the Barren Lands. The snow had wrapped the sharp edges of every ridge in a sheer blanket that stretched for a thousand miles, undulating in slow and glistening waves to the hard line of a distant horizon. It shone—a domain of death—where so late the wild rose blossomed and the air throbbed with innumerable wings.

The man halted, slackened his shoulders, and sat for a moment on the pack-sack. He had come twenty miles and another twenty remained to be traversed. He felt no fatigue; the muscles in his body were like well-oiled steel springs. Presently he stood up, stretched his arms, resumed his load, and swung down-hill towards the nearest thicket of spruce. Here—taking off his shoes—he built a small fire, made tea, and ate sparingly of pork and bread. Both being frozen solid, he scorched them, meditatively, at the end of a stick.

He remained thus for half an hour, his strong jaws champing, and tossing a morsel now and then to a jay who lit suddenly on a branch nearby. Its head was tilted on one side, while, chattering sharply, it regarded him with bright, inquisitive eyes. He rubbed a wisp of tobacco in his palm, smoked for a few moments, then, knocking the ice from the webbing of his shoes, thrust his feet into the straps and swung on. Just at this moment there came to him on the wind a faint sound from beyond the ridge.

"My God!" he said under his breath.

An hour later he was five miles away, walking fast. His face was set, and a hard light glinted in his frosty eyes. Now and again he glanced over his shoulder—quick, furtive glances that seemed to shrink from finding what they sought. The sound came less intermittently—clearer and nearer—the most terrible voice in the North—the voice of the terror of the wilderness.

Soon afterwards he saw them—like black specks that moved steadily over a white counterpane—

two miles away, but distinct in the glittering air. In single file they travelled, the tall leader lifting now and then her black muzzle and sending out a note of death—the hunting call of the pack. It drifted through the desolation. Fur and feather heard and knew it. Mink and marten tunnelled into the snow, the rabbit scampered to his burrow, and even carcajou—the wolverine—scuffled hastily for shelter.

The man, too, heard it and cursed. From the mouth of his pack-sack projected the sawed-off muzzle of a Winchester rifle. He unstrapped this and tested the magazine. There were three cartridges. His lips pressed tight and, glancing ahead, he strode off with quickened pace towards a clump of small timber that lay in a depression half a mile ahead. Once there he slipped off his burden. The voice of the pack was nearer now.

Selecting the largest spruce, he chopped off the lower branches to a height of six feet, leaving a series of sharp points. Then, swinging the sack into the tree, he mounted swiftly, his rifle slung over his shoulder. Ten minutes later a grey wolf loped noiselessly by, smelt at the trampled snow and squatted on her haunches. In the next moment the green eyes were fastened on the man.

The long black muzzle opened and the call went forth—sharp and terrible. Came an answering whimper from the thicket and six more wolves trotted up, their gaunt frames moving with incredible smoothness. There was no sound save wind in the tree-tops and the soft muffled thud as some laden branch deposited its weight of snow. The seven beasts stared up and the man stared down. They were all full grown, but the bitch that led them was the biggest of all, with long flanks, deep hairy chest, clean, sharp, black muzzle and pointed ears. She spoke once, and the pack squatted, noses between forepaws, the fur deep on the ridges of their backs, the lips lifted a little, the green eyes fixed in a remorseless stare. They could afford to wait.

The man shifted gingerly to another branch. Instantly the seven brutes were erect, their backs bristling. The grey leader licked her dark muzzle, while from her shaggy throat came a warning note. Very slowly he pulled the Winchester from its case. When he looked down again the pack had scattered and circled with soundless feet fifty yards away, slipping like wraiths from tree to tree, visible one moment, invisible the next, implacable and restless, with death locked in their jaws. He perceived that it was useless to shoot. One could not kill a ghost.

The wind strengthened, till all around there was a swaying of thick green branches and a tumbling of snow. The patrol did not slacken. A little clear glade lay southward, and beyond he could see open country—wind-smitten—devoid of life. It was an hour when all that lived on the Barren Lands sought shelter, save only the grey terror of the wilds.

Rigid on his perch the cold began to strike more formidably. He felt it first in hands and feet, and knocked them together noisily, whereat there was a closing in of the savage ring and a sharper gleam in the merciless eyes. He continued his movements till the tree was surrounded by a cordon of jaws, when suddenly he snatched at his rifle and fired.

There was a scattering of padded feet and the tall bitch dragged one leg, while she yelped fury and revenge. The man laid his rifle carefully across a branch. He had two cartridges left. His brows were pulled down, his arms and legs were getting numb, the cold was reaching his body. He drew off one mitt and pressed his palm against a frost-bite on his cheek. He slipped a little, recovering himself with a queer feeling of sickness.

The light began to fade. Followed that amazingly short period when in these latitudes darkness seems to pour from the sky and crush out the day. The sky turned red, pink, grey, till a hard purple asserted itself. The evening star hung like a lamp low over the horizon. Simultaneously the pack found courage, closing in till the gaunt bodies were almost beneath him, as though they knew that he had but two cartridges left and was keeping one for himself.

The tall bitch stood upright on hind-legs and scratched at the frozen bark with extended claws. He could look straight down her throat. How black was the roof of her mouth! There was no yelping now, but only an occasional quick, light panting of the deep chests. They had settled down to wait.

The man's thighs grew stiff where they gripped the tree. His back and shoulders had lost all heat, and he felt the drowsiness that in the North heralds the approach of one's last sleep. It came to him that he must not wait too long, or he would be alive when he tumbled. He felt again at the Winchester. This time the pack did not move. Very carefully he lowered the butt of the rifle till it rested on a lifeless foot. Then he drew the muzzle vertically under his chin.

A wolf on the outskirts of the circle put his nose into the air with a querulous whimper. Something in the sound of it galvanised his grey brethren into stiff attention. They stood like images, the wind lifting their long hair, their pointed ears rigid. Another whimper, and another, till suddenly the pack wheeled and raced like phantoms down the glade.

The man, his rifle still in position, strained his smarting eyes. A mile away, where the white plain glistened beneath a full moon, he saw a cluster of dark bodies ploughing laboriously through the drifts. It was a band of coast caribou. The pack made for them, every throat flinging terrible cries into the night.

He waited for five minutes, then another five. Presently he dropped his pack-sack and half-slid, half-tumbled from his perch. He could not feel the toe-straps of his shoes. Standing for a moment to make sure of the wind's direction, he broke into a half-trot, trailing the rifle and heading down-wind. A spruce partridge cheeped sleepily in an adjoining tree. A mink pushed his head out of a crevice and stole light-footed to the stain of blood that shone like a ruby on the sparkling snow.

II

Ten miles away another man dragged himself slowly southward. The sinews of his legs were burning like fire. For hours he had tramped, travelling by the lie of the land and the run of hidden rivers, but now the punishment of the trail was on him, the trail that tempts and tortures, that allures and kills, the trail to which the hearts of men respond as to a trumpet-call.

He had ten miles to go, but his food was exhausted. Matches he had in a tight box with a screw cap, and an axe. Ten miles back he had taken a wrong turn that led him through rough country where no man was meant to go. One shoe was broken. He had patched it up and tramped on, but his fingers were too stiff for fine work, and the frame gave at every step.

The pain in his legs increased, and he grew hungry. The fact, rather than the hunger, made him clench his lips and push on though every step was agony. He knew that to be hungry is to be cold, that to be cold is to be weak, and that for those who are weak the North has no mercy. He fired once at a rabbit and missed, his fingers being too stiff to manipulate the trigger.

His mind began to work queerly. It seemed to him that the North was like a mistress—beautiful but heartless—winning men's souls, then destroying them. Always, it appeared, this mistress did nothing. The men themselves did everything—theirs being the pride, the passion, and the offering. Then, when she had taken everything, she just waited with that wintry smile of hers, and the end came very quickly. She did not change, being assured of interminable lovers from all corners of the earth who would in turn make their oblations and receive their grim reward.

Presently the pain became so great that he knew that he must rest, no matter how that rest might end, and just at that moment he saw ahead of him a stretch of glare ice where a river wound southward. He struck down-hill thankfully. Reaching the ice, he still wore his shoes so as to distribute weight, and moved on. His legs did not hurt so much now, being relieved from lifting that weary webbing. He was looking at the line of scanty timber along the shore, when everything gave way beneath. Automatically he spread out his arms.

He was immersed neck-deep in a chilling flood whose current tugged invisibly at the great shoes as though trying to rip them off. He twisted at them, but his mittens slipped on the glare ice and the effort merely drew him under. The current clutched his body, and through it there crept the first assault of breathless cold. He gasped sharply, seeming to have no feet left.

Presently he tried again, staring at the shore, which seemed so near and warm and unapproachable. He shouted, emptying his lungs, but heard only the drone of wind and the intense frost at work in the scanty timber, with sharp rifle-like reports that died with dwindling echoes down far stretches of the manacled river. Then he knew that he must save himself—or die.

Twisting desperately, and pressing hard with his arms on the yielding ice, he turned his body up-stream and, pointing his toes downwards, he felt one foot, then the other, loosen. Another twist and his ankles came free. The blind current took the shoes swiftly. He rested a moment, and, with a grim smile, thrust one arm into the water and laid it dripping on the ice. Then the other.

In a few seconds he was anchored—congealed and riveted there—a portion of a man—as though in supplication to some unknown god. He began to pull, crooking elbows. His shoulders lifted. There sounded a warning crack, but his breast was by now over the edge. He drew a long, shivering breath and pulled again.

This time his thighs came up. He crawled a few feet forward, the only wet thing in that bitter wilderness, but wet only for an instant. His clothing ceased to drip and became armour, stiffening momentarily, and gripping his exhausted body where no heat was. He began to shuffle arduously to the shore, crackling as he went — half-man, half-animal — seeking the shelter of the woods.

Reaching them gasping, he broke open his pocket and pulled at the match-box he could no longer feel. It was more difficult to get at his axe, the haft of which hung at his belt, its head in a leather pouch. His mittens refused to grasp it. He clutched with frozen hands, making cuts at dead trees, breaking dry twigs, stamping the snow. The cold had nearly reached his heart. He got the box open by holding the cap in his teeth, and finally lit a match by biting its head. This he pushed under a handful of birch-bark and stood breathless, swinging his arms.

His circulation quickened a little. Savage spots developed in face, hands and feet, where frost had struck deep. He lengthened the fire, heaping it high, then set to work building another six feet distant. Between them he toiled like a salamander, his clothing now dripping. Eight feet away it was forty below zero.

Ten minutes later he began to strip off his now softened armour, spreading it on branches stuck upright in the sodden snow. It steamed furiously, and he tended it in bare feet, clad only in drawers. There was a roaring of flames, a crackling of wood. In this recess the wind did not reach him, but he was alternately baked and frozen as he moved towards or from the twin furnaces. Heat blisters spread amongst the frost-bites, and his skin looked like mottled marble. In half an hour he smelt scorched cloth and dressed quickly. Here and there the clothing was burnt through, but it was dry. His moccasins took the longest. Finally he gave this up and put them on, when they instantly became hard, like parchment.

He struck out for the river-bank, wading through

snow that came nearly to his middle. At the edge of the ice he paused, scanned the black spot where a glaze had already formed over an irregular hole, and began to struggle down-stream, trusting to the ice as much as he dared, but clinging nevertheless within reach of the friendly shore.

III

To the west of the river lifted a medley of ridges, ironed smooth by the snow. On the other side of this a third man moved southward. From a mountain-top it would have been seen that the trails of all three travellers converged towards the same point, where from a cluster of dark green timber a thin grey pencil of smoke climbed into the keen air. It was a throb of life in the wilderness, a magnet to the wanderers, a place of warmth and food.

The third man progressed uncertainly, diverging now and then from the faint depression left by the swinging tread of some former traveller. He was tall and gaunt. His sunken cheeks were grey with frost, ice plastered his feet, and he walked with a strangely uncertain step, stopping now and then to rub his eyes and peer questioningly at the driven snow ahead.

He had been tramping thus since early morning. At noon his eyes began to smart and at two o'clock the rims of the lids were red and swoollen; an hour later they began to stick, while a thick, glutinous fluid oozed from their stinging corners. The flesh around them swelled rapidly, and they burnt as though seared with hot irons.

He pushed on drunkenly, swaying as he went, but ever the interminable glitter of the snow struck upward and smote him the more fiercely. The trail grew dim. Trees passed like men walking. His ears, sharpened by distress, became his interpreters, bringing him the faint squeak of small startled animals and a heavy beat of wings as an ivory-beaked raven winnowed the air overhead. The whiteness of the land grew blurred, and his lips moved in a wordless petition. He walked now as one who sees with his feet, feeling for the slight hardness of the trail, the light of day being for him as darkness. Then his lids refused to be rubbed open, and he did not see anything any more.

He stood for a little while quite still, feeling with moistened fingers to establish what wind might blow. His face expressed no fear, but just a dumb wonder that this thing should have come to him. There were so many other men abroad in the North. Suddenly it struck him that he had been a fool not to stop an hour ago and make some kind of camp and fire. That was what he wanted now—fire.

He stamped with his shoes to make sure he was on the trail; then, to make doubly sure, took off his mitts and felt beneath the light surface drift for the thickened shell that should lie just below. He found it unmistakably, and nodded. In the very middle of it he began to dig, using one shoe as a shovel and casting into the wind. Three feet down he came to moss and, poking at arm's height, determined that his parapet was nearly level with his head. He stood now in a hole some four feet square, with sharply sloping sides. Testing the wind again, he found none.

By this time he was used to the dark, though his eyes hurt more than ever, and, opening his pack-sack—fumbling a little with the straps—he pulled out a pair of Hudson Bay blankets. Wrapping these round his body, he thrust himself in as far as he could beneath the parapet, allowing the displaced snow to cover him completely. As it slid over his face, which was nearly hidden by a capote, he put out a hand, holding it stiffly till the slide ceased. The hand was presently withdrawn to inner darkness, leaving an irregular air-hole a few inches long. There was left but a depression, from which spurted small regular puffs of vapour. Beside it a pair of wide shoes stood up into the wind, and at the bottom lay a half-emptied pack-sack.

The moon came out, the cold intensified. In the pale light rabbits hopped, like bundles of white fur with large pink eyes. An Arctic owl circled with wide, noiseless pinions above the hole, like a ghost of the wilderness. An otter came streaking up the trail, which here ran close to the river, leaving a narrow furrow in the loose drift. Carcajou—the wolverine and glutton—stared at the pack-sack, then slid down and began tearing it to pieces with strong white teeth, till suddenly the jets of vapour caught his small black eyes, and he scrambled back in a paroxysm of fear.

The moon swam majestically naked through a sky sown with innumerable stars, casting blue-black shadows where the scattered spruce dotted the lower land. The river, like a strip of polished glass, wound southward—its surface whipped clear of snow. There was no sound save the steady drone from the North—a potent voice that through the winter months holds its interminable pitch. In this abode of solitude, peopled by fur and feather wise in the law of the wilderness and waging the endless war for existence, man survives only by the stoutness of his heart and the strength of his body. The battle is to the strong. The wind bites, the cold pierces, the way of the trail is arduous, and he who falters is doomed. It is a stark country, grim and unforgiving, merciless in its mandates and swift to punish.

Far up the trail a dark figure became visible, moving fast with long, swinging tread, bending forward in the attitude of the practised walker, It was the first man, with strength flowing its full warm tide through his sinewy frame. His eyes were bright and he thought not at all of what had been, but of a log cabin farther down the river, where a lamp would be burning in the window beneath the laden roof. Quickly he came, till, opposite the shoes, he stopped abruptly and stared down at the torn pack-sack. As he stared it seemed that very faintly there issued from the snow itself a fine, intermittent vapour.

With an exclamation he twisted his feet free and began to dig.

Ten minutes later he was working desperately over a stiff body stretched beside a blazing fire. His methods were harsh but efficacious. The breath began to reinhabit the lungs it had so nearly deserted. Presently the blind man sighed deeply and a quiver ran through his frame. At that the rescuer redoubled his efforts, and, lifting the slack shoulders, put a steaming cup to the blue lips.

"Hard luck!" he said. "Drink this."

They started an hour afterwards, the rescuer in the lead. Behind him, and grasping the end of a raw-hide tump-line, came the saved—walking uncertainly, with weak knees and wavering feet. The man in front was carrying both pack-sacks, which loomed up mountainously in the pale white light. He stopped now and again with a word of encouragement, asking no questions, but his brain worked for them both.

At the second bend of the river he stopped. The blind man heard, and halted at once, his ears accomplishing a double duty. The rescuer peered at the river, where it seemed something was moving, mysteriously uncouth. He slung his Winchester forward and felt for the trigger, then, with a grunt, let the weapon lie loose in his arm.

Two hundred yards away a man was floundering in the snow, his arms waving despairingly. He was nearly spent, falling often and rising to his feet, plastered with white—half-engulfed in the sparkling sea around him. He tried to shout, but could make only a half-choked, inarticulate sound, more beast-like than human. On he came, wallowing towards the trail. The first man stood, till suddenly the truth was clear and he stepped swiftly forward. A moment later the stranger pitched on his face and lay still.

An hour passed. The blind man heard one voice, then two, the second being weak and almost incoherent. He caught words of encouragement, smelt a fire, and moved on as close as he dared. He was too far gone to talk himself, but knew that mercy walked abroad that night in the Barren Lands. After a while someone spoke to him in tones he knew:

"We'll start now. Stamp down as hard as you can—this fellow has no shoes."

The three got into motion—and the second man—the blind one—held thankfully on to the tump-line. He heard the shoes of the leader driven down on to the trail by legs of piston-like force, and stamped weakly himself, numbly conscious that uncertain steps were following close behind. There was no talk—breath being too precious to consume in speech.

The last man mustered all his strength. His body, savagely frost-bitten, felt as though burnt by hot metal, his legs and thighs were wound with ribbons of pain. Snow was plastered on his face, and in the small of his neck throbbed the one warning signal which the men of the North have learnt to heed—the protest of a body that is about to revolt. He did not think much of his own distress, but of the one in front. That was hard luck.

The blind man pushed on with dwindling force. His closed eyes exuded a paste that froze on his wind-whipped cheeks. His very spine felt frozen. It was queer to be walking in the dark between two strangers. What sort of a time, he wondered, had the last man experienced! His own eyes would be better in a few days, but it was tough to be out in the woods without snowshoes.

The first man walked slowly, moderating his pace to suit the others. He had noted the ghastly look on the features of the last one rescued, and the face stuck in his mind. It was tough to go through the ice in weather like this, and tougher still to have to sacrifice one's shoes. He was glad he had never been caught like that. As to the blind one he felt even more sorry. It was worse to be helpless than to be half-frozen. He spoke over his shoulder occasionally—watching to see that he was not going too fast. Presently—straight ahead—a spark of yellow light glowed through the dark of a clump of trees. He gave one great, joyful shout.

• • • • •

For twelve hours the three lay motionless in bunks built one over the other. The first man was on top—the blind one at the bottom. The former awoke and blinked at the red-hot stove, stuffed with blazing wood. The roar of it and the weight of blankets over him were both grateful. He lay for a little while, smoking peacefully, then, hearing movements beneath, put his head over the wooden sideboard and looked down.

"Hallo, pilgrim, how goes it?"

The third man grunted comfortably. "Fine!" Then he too leant out and surveyed the occupant of the bottom bunk.

"How do you feel, partner?"

The blind man stretched a pair of mottled arms. His face was still plastered with the discharge from closed and swollen lids.

"Like a bull moose. Do I smell coffee?"

THE CIRCUIT OF THE WILD SWAN

Along the shore of a palm-fringed lagoon two black swans moved slowly, and from their curving breasts spread a double ripple that died with a whisper against the land. Above them a tropic moon shed a pale glory in which they seemed like slender ships floating through a dream. The stars were large and lustrous, the air full of nameless murmurs that breathed delicately from swamp and jungle.

Presently the stroke of the wide, webbed feet quickened as, from far ahead, came a cluster of great birds flying low, their whipping wings just clearing the black surface of the water, till, with a sudden splashing and furrowing of the hitherto unbroken expanse, they came to rest close beside.

Months before they had arrived from the North, weary with buffeting the winds of seven thousand miles, the tip feathers of their pinions broken, their muscles lean and stiff. But since then there was rest and safety and love-making and rearing of young and feeding on soft-shell fish and sweet, bulbous things with which the shore of the lagoon was bordered, and in this period the thin bodies filled out, the worn feathers became smooth and lustrous, and the strong mandibles grew hard and bright.

For a day they floated, listening intently for the

mysterious call they would instantly obey. There were two trumpeters, snow-white save for the black tips to their wing feathers, black mandibles and feet, and reddish eyes; four great dark birds, blue-black and dun-coloured, with yellow eyes and thick, rough mandibles that projected like lumps from their black skulls; and two grey swans of a rusty white, with buff-yellow feet and breasts, and beady eyes with black pupil and grey iris. In pairs they had spent the past luxurious month, but now congregated, with crooning and low, soft whistles and sharp trumpeting, for a brief and communicative space.

It was the next night when the call came. There followed a redoubled exchange in voices smooth and rough, and a series of trial flights in which the blue-black leader spiralled high and tested the wind that came, hot and oppressive, from the equator. At his swiftly won elevation he caught innumerable whispers from the South. Then the others climbed their five thousand feet into the humid air, after which there were circlings, seemingly aimless, but all dominated by the strange wisdom of the speechless. Finally the leader swung off with a calm certitude in the beat of his mighty pinions, and one by one the rest of the hurtling birds swerved into a swaying wedge that, mounting higher and higher, threaded the thin air with increasing speed.

In three hours they had traversed two hundred and fifty miles, and were well out over the Caribbean, holding west of north and paralleling the Lesser Antilles. At a height of two miles the air was fresh and cool, and beneath them a vast plain of sea lay crisping against the velvet of scattered islands in leagues of lacy foam. By this time the wedge had taken up its appointed order, the order it would hold for the Arctic. At the apex throbbed the black leader, his long neck straight and stiff, his bright eyes half sheathed against the whistling wind, his wings hollowed to the most efficient curve, cutting his liquid way with unvarying velocity. At his right flank flew his mate, and behind her the four swans, trumpeter and grey. On the other side sped the great dun-coloured birds, each flinging its pulsing body into the partial vacuum left by its predecessor. Lifting under the press of upward currents, dipping into air-pockets, yielding almost imperceptibly to the side thrust of an unsteady wind, the streaming phalanx sped on with the rhythmical throb of rapidly beating wings.

Five hundred miles from the South American coast a tremor of expectation ran through the flock. A little more and they would begin a long slant that always ended beside a certain sheltered key that lies between Guadeloupe and Porto Rico, a key beloved of feathered voyagers at a season of the year. But just as the extended necks craned downward there came out of the east an angry gust, and mysteriously the air beneath them became full of ragged clouds.

Instantly the pilot swung to the right, till, breasting the first heralds of bad weather, he shot his sleek body against the strengthening wind, testing its force and receiving in his tingling ears quick, warning messages from the grey Atlantic. The wedge followed him, with a little widening of formation, a little slackening of effort till, assured of an approaching gale, the master mariner of this viewless ocean struck up a swift incline that lifted the flock to fifteen thousand feet. Then, supported, as it were, by the upper fringes of the storm, he swerved westward and laid his course for Haiti. Here, in a long bay on Enriquilla Lake, the travellers rested. They had come a thousand miles in twelve hours.

Now, of the jaunt across Cuba to the Floridian swamps, and of the long but luxurious glide up the Gulf of Mexico to the marshes of Alabama, it is not necessary to write, for day after day innumerable leaders guide their kinsmen through these high and uncharted spaces till the air above is as a travelled road. And even by night-time, if the skies are clear and the winds favourable, we may descry these distant pilgrims, their microscopic bodies seemingly threading a hazardous way between the stars. But when the dun-coloured swan saw the lights of Tampa on the horizon he sent out a deep-throated "coo-whoo, coo-whoo," that rang like a silver bugle, and was answered distantly by other and invisible voyagers through the semi-tropical dusk, while all around him the air was filled with the soft winnowing of tireless wings.

Disaster waited farther north. Remembering of old that at the first Great Lake there was a place that made him nervous when he passed over it at whatever height, the leader held to the west, meaning to avoid the territory of great smoke and follow up the west shore of Lake Michigan. But, fifty miles south of Chicago, he ran into a gale that thrust him eastward. With it came a late snowfall. Whirring through the grey plain of cloud, he mounted above the blizzard to altitudes where the air was piercingly cold, while the flock, stiff and weary after long flight, complained in querulous voices that they would be compelled, and that soon, to descend in an untested country.

Two hours afterward the leader craned his dark neck and slid downward at a mile and a half a minute. Through a wrinkle in the cloud he had caught a patch of grey, and since grey in springtime means water, while black, at all times of the year, means danger, he flung himself onward with utmost velocity. They skimmed over woods, the branches of which were unseasonably white, and over a wide, flat place where they passed directly above a brown speck that saw them and barked furiously. At last, close underneath, was the water, looking smooth and oily as the snowflakes touched it and vanished.

That evening the great birds rested on the icy lake, their necks double-curved close against their snow-covered shoulders, while the dun pilot kept watch. He too was very tired, but his yellow eyes stared unceasingly into the dark, and he swam slowly to and fro, trailing his wide, webbed feet. A little later it appeared that the snow thickened just in one direction. He moved toward this with sudden suspicion, till when, quite close and fifty yards ahead of the others, a dull knock sounded with startling distinctness. Instantly he perceived danger, and with one shrill alarm dived directly for the point of peril. Not two feet under the water, and with his tail-feathers still exposed, he heard a noise like thunder. Four times it came and with it flashes of red lightning. At that he struck out more desperately, and, rising to the surface behind the strange snowbank, clattered into the air. Then, mounting a thousand feet, he flew round and round in swift and anxious circles. But down below an excited farmer, after breaking the beautiful neck of the pilot's crippled mate by the stroke of his swinging oar, dragged her, with the twitching bodies of the two remaining black swans, into the flat bottom of his cotton-shrouded punt.

A week later the diminished wedge slackened its speed and slid comfortably a few thousand feet to lower altitudes. Beneath them the barren lands unfolded toward the Arctic, a country whose naked ribs projected irregularly from the moss-covered surface, a vast tundra of rocks, lakes and troubled rivers, smitten in winter by hard winds that whistled from the pole, and for a brief summer bursting into a wild opulence of flower and fruit. Here, in the Athabasca area, was the home of the swans. On bare promontories they lived or on tiny islets where the crystal waters lap close to the nest, itself a few sticks or a wisp of grass lined with down plucked from parental breasts. The dun-coloured leader had wedded beside the lagoon of British Guiana, but his young had gone their own way and left him lonely. Now, with strange memories of a bitter and fatal life, he suddenly resigned his mastership, and, quickening his pace, began a long and solitary patrol of the lonely and rocky shore, while the others, trumpeter and grey, winged a deliberate course to their own well-remembered quarters.

Presently the wanderer, sailing low, drifted over a nest where a graceful black swan nestled close while her mate fished contentedly in a nearby marsh. At the intruder's approach there set up a shrill whistling that brought an infuriated bird to a vicious defence of home and country. The battle that followed was Homeric, with a fierce arching of sinewy necks, a sharp hissing from gaping mandibles, and quick, deadly strokes of great, scythe-like wings. The female did not move. It all seemed to her somehow quite suitable that battle-royal be waged over her sleek person, so she only ruffled her soft breast feathers, curved her neck into more graceful lines than ever, and prepared to pay swan-like homage to the victor. In another moment her mate lifted himself heavily into the air. The dun-coloured pilot, still savage over the catastrophe of the week before, was irresistible. Now he glanced redly at the dwindling outline of the vanquished, and, with a triumphant flutter of mighty wings and a deep, soft note of love in his blue-black throat, marched exulting to his prize.

Then came lengthening and luxurious days during which the sun grew warmer, and the wrens, finches, yellow-hammers, and all the short-beaked and cross-beaked tribe fluttered, twittering, over the land in dancing flights of wind-blown colour. Beneath the breast of the brooding swan were two great, mottled, slaty eggs, over which she spread a protecting body while she watched her captor swimming nearby, jerking up swan-root with its sweet, carrot-shaped bulb, and shell-fish, and, best of all, the pink shrimp that began to drift in careless schools along the barren shore. At times he winged slowly across the lake to a low point where assembled daily that strangest of all Northern gatherings, the club or conclave of male swans. Hither, from near and far, the great birds journeyed, leaving their mates to domestic duties, and joined in a shrill and strenuous symposium. Here too, by ancient law, might approach no feminine visitor save she whom adversity or the kestrel hawk had robbed of her husband. In this case she came, a prey to unaccustomed loneliness, to select from the club members a second spouse. And at her advent there was redoubled clamour and a preening of lustrous feathers, till, with a whistle of relief, she rose into the air and turned homeward with a flattered companion.

By the end of June the cygnets were born, two naked and shapeless things with gigantic, bony heads and angular wings that bore sproutings of incipient quills. Over them the parents lavished the gleanings of the lake, till their pink and quivering bodies bulged with food. Now, too, was constant warfare with mink and otter that crept, dripping, from the shore, and with white foxes, tarnished to a dirty yellow, that made swift raids from scanty cover. In the air there were hurried flights from wheeling hawks, whose sharp beaks hovered perilously near the great birds' defenceless backs, while carcajou, the wolverine, braved the hissing mandibles for one gulp of a delicious and featherless morsel. Anxious weeks were these, but all the time the cygnets grew larger and stronger, and their grotesque proportions became more familiar, till, with young plumage half-developed, they swayed uncertainly to the water's edge and found, to their amazement, that they could swim.

The tension lessened after that, for each day added to their powers. Simultaneously it seemed that the lake was wrinkled with new broods of swan, geese and ducks. There were geese, grey and white, the latter the clear-throated wavy that undulates so swiftly in its flight; black ducks with heavy, barrel-like bodies and short, strong wings; mallards in grey, green and scarlet; wood duck, resplendent with crested cowls and shimmering, painted breasts; blue teal, whose whirring course was bullet-like; widgeon, whistlers, cranes, and great mergansers with sharp-pointed bills and saw-like teeth that caught fish and tossed them, glittering, in the air. All through the day they talked, and far into the night, and then, when sleep overtook them, the Northern loon unleashed his weird laughter and flung it, echoing, to the stars. So for a space, while the stiff earth relaxed her ageless limbs, the hot flare of sun called forth a prodigal fertility of fruit and flower, and the winged life of the Barren Lands approached its most strange and perilous period.

In August the older birds began to moult, and before long lost much of their winter plumage. This, wind-whipped and worn, had never recovered from the stress of pilgrimage, and now the great wing-feathers, one by one, were displaced by the prickly thrust of new quills beneath the toughened skin. In this guise the swans became doubly helpless. Flight was denied them, and only unceasing care and a searching out of sheltered places saved them from the assault of a multitude of enemies. They seemed a strangely hybrid breed, leading a precarious existence on land and water, their garb a motley patchwork through which their fat bodies showed irregularly in islands of pink and roughened flesh. Then, in the early autumn, when the hasty fruit of the North is at its fullest, and when the wild things finding subsistence easy are indolent and surfeited, the half-fledged birds began their journey to the coast.

By land and water they travelled, here swimming, here waddling strenuously with lumbering gait and taut, stretched, anxious necks. Their skins were tingling with the new growth that not yet could carry them aloft, but deep in their flat skulls moved an ancient wisdom. Not by fresh fruit and fresh-water food could they attain the strength they would shortly need, when the message came from the upper air, but only by the sharp sea taste of shell-fish from the salt sands of the bitter water. Of no purport for a journey was the soft flesh of mating- and breeding-time, and it was not written that a brooding swan might rise from her nest or her companion wing straightway from his club and both reel off untiring leagues of space. Thus, in the appointed hour, from tarn and lake, from promontory, point and island, the half-feathered folk turned to their life-giving mother, the sea. Toward her they flowed in an ever-increasing stream, choosing hidden paths where, defenceless, they pushed through narrow lanes of grey caribou moss or among sparse growths, that the white fox, peering from his hole, might not descry their arduous passage. In scanty thickets the wood buffalo raised his blunt and shaggy head, and often, across the far-flung tundra, they saw vast herds carpeting the plain, with multitudes of round, barrel-like bodies, while on the skyline the grey wolf stalked in restless patrol, waiting for the deer that, outcast by age or disease, would inevitably fall to his merciless jaws.

But long ere the journey was ended the old swans' wing-feathers were full grown, and the cygnets had mastered the first elements of flight. The latter travelled unevenly in bursts of speed that ended with abrupt bumps on the moss-covered plain, while their parents circled overhead, uttering warning and encouraging cries. A delightful procession this, with the thin air like wine, with the barren lands mapped below, stretching in dwindling miles out of sight, and the call of the sea sounding ever more clearly across the horizon. In it the young birds were taught many things that pertained to their amazing art: how to glide from beneath the swoop of the Northern kite—for the swan is, above all fliers, defenceless; how to dive in the green water and change course the moment one's tail-feathers were out of sight; how to take cover so that one's long neck did not project with uncomfortable distinction. There were feastings, too, on ripe cranberries that shone in scarlet clusters along the creek bottoms, and on blueberries, sweet and purple, where often they found the black bear sitting on his haunches, while his forearms gathered the laden bushes to his hairy breast. So eastward they fared, convoyed by other flocks, whose mingled salutations rang cheerily through the hollow skies, till on a day there came a sharpness in the atmosphere and beneath them lay the grey shield of the Northern Ocean, rimmed by endless leagues of glistening and mud-coloured shore.

Here, it seemed, the life of the North had congregated for that brief but luxurious period which precedes the frost. The polar bear buried his sharp snout in the quivering side of a white whale stranded by the lowering tide, and, at a little distance, loitered the grey wolves till the masters of the North be satisfied. Behind the wolves peered the bright pink eyes of the Arctic fox, scavengers of the shore, and still farther down the scale the mink and marten bided their time till their soft pads might sink unnoted toward the feast. Divers and loons fished continually, and the broad-billed tribes thrust their mandibles into delicious heaps of seaweed, finding crabs and sea-worms, the very taste of which filled the hungry birds with strange and sudden yearnings for flight. Over the flat waters wheeled flocks of gulls, while, farther out, the rounded back of the rorqual glinted in the sun, or a school of speeding porpoise flashed into the air, sprinkling diamonds of prismatic light. Life was here, young life, bursting with crescent power that flushed and surged, growing stronger and more riotous ere it should join the stern test that would begin with the first whirring flakes of snow.

The season drew on. By night and day rose the clamour of the feathered folk, for in these proving grounds soft muscles were growing tough and strong, and the fat crops that so late were stuffed with fruit now became cleansed and hard with salt sand, whereby the marvellous digestion of the broad-billed people is attained. Short beaks and cross-beaks had long since disappeared, and there was left nothing that twittered or sang. Old pilots, wise of wind and weather, mounted high, and after them streamed inconsequent flocks of young birds, ignorant of the law and rejoicing in new-found powers. Far up, where the air was thin, they followed, only to discover that youth had much to learn and these latitudes were full of invisible forces that buffeted and played with them, dropping them into pockets and tilting them with savage gusts till, weary of the sport, they sank earthward with wild and raucous protests, while their leaders sailed, serene and unshaken, in the zenith. But gradually these excursions took on definite form. Youth learned experience, and instinct asserted its rule. Three weeks after the dun-coloured leader reached salt water, the teeming populace of the shore was ready to migrate.

It happened that this was a year of false alarms, in which the chill breath of the North was intermittent and gave way, as though relenting, to successive days of sunshine and warmth. Once and again the great black swan, mounting high into the uncertain air-lanes, and deciding that the hour had come, had marshalled his pointed squadron, only to be baffled by lenient breezes that crept up from the South. But when night fell there was a tightening along the shore and a glint on the pools that he marked with blinking eye and tested with his webbed feet. On one of these mornings the ducks departed, and, as silence set in, he listened tensely for that first unmistakable message of the Arctic.

Presently it came, with a little shifting of the wind and a little shudder from the sea. The grey waters took on an aspect empty and bleak, while the ripples that crisped the margin of the bay seemed to have become almost metallic. The surface of the water ceased to reflect the low-lying clouds, and stretched, dull and burnished, with strange suggestions of molten fluid. Then, as though loosed by dainty, invisible fingers, there danced from the North a few flakes of starry snow.

Hardly had they reached him, when there fell upon the hooded ear of the black swan a fine and steady drone. At that he waited no more, but, clattering upward, flung a signal to the little group of voyagers whose long necks and bright eyes had turned to him inquiringly for days past. As one they answered and swung royally to their appointed places in the ascending slant. Two miles above the sea the pilot wheeled twice, quickening his pace in magnificent circles, till, poising for an instant at Olympian heights, this wise and valiant bird gathered the winds of Æolus into the booming curve of his mighty pinions and struck off on the superb line of his long, uncharted course.

THE BLINDNESS OF PITULUK

STEERING north by west up Baffin's Strait, and passing Amadjauk Harbour on the east, with Salisbury Island well into the south, you will make Cape Dorset. That is, if you are weather-wise and succeed in bucking through the ice-pack. Farther north comes the big bend that turns into Fox Channel—and so to Greenland waters.

From the naked ribs of Baffin Land, Cape Dorset thrusts a gigantic thumb into the cool, green ocean. Past its rubbed and fretted apex streams annually a great procession, belched, grinding, from the Arctic. Month after month it ramps by, broken occasionally into pond-like gaps where the square flipper suns himself on the trembling floe, and the dark-eyed jar seal falls prey to white bears marooned and adrift on the tumbled plain.

At all this, Pituluk, a lean Husky, had gazed calmly for years. In winter his igloo huddled low in a wrinkle of the shore. In summer his topeck crowned a little ridge from which the water ran both ways when it rained. And with him lived Tuktu, the Caribou, and Kugyiyuk, the Swan.

They were old, friendless and decrepit, but not in any way impressed by the fact that they owed these declining years to the good nature of Pituluk. Tuktu was lame and had a withered arm and a nasty, complaining temper; while Kugyiyuk, even older than her husband, was something like a piece of sinew that has been left out in the sun. What Pituluk, a large, easygoing man, gave them they took as if it were a right, and when food was scanty, as not infrequently happened, they bombarded him with complaint and criticism that seemed to slide like drops of rain from his oily skin.

Kugyiyuk had black eyes that shifted as though greased in their sockets, and stumps of ancient, rusty teeth whose strength had long since vanished with much tugging at sinew and gnawing at the edges of walrus-hides.

In the warm weather Pituluk fished for salmon, and shot white foxes as they feasted on dead whales driven ashore by the run of Arctic currents. Sometimes he faced a she-bear that lounged forth, lean and vicious, with the cub she had suckled for months in a snow-covered crevice. There was no difficulty about summer. The caribou were fat, and his guests better tempered.

But when winter arrived with Unorri, the North Wind, both land and sea tightened up like the snapping of the lock in a Hudson Bay musket, and the ragged outlines of beach and ridge were smoothed down and plastered over. As soon as he could find packed snow, Pituluk built his igloo, and then began the long yearly struggle against the gods of the out-of-doors. The foxes lost the mangy, blue tinge of earlier months, becoming blenched like ice and hard to see. The salmon backed into deep water. The caribou retreated inland, and the square flipper came up to breathe in places not easy to find. And when one walked abroad, it often happened that one saw only the great form of a solitary he-bear, rocking his arrow-shaped head as he stalked out to the edge of the ice to fish.

In such times Tuktu and Kugyiyuk were hard to live with. The old woman reckoned her years by the number of times she had seen the pack-ice march down from Boothia Gulf. Seventy-five times she made it. Tuktu was nearly as old. Staring at them as he sat on the snow ledge of his house, mending a spear, Pituluk wondered why the aged should become so cross. They had nothing to do but eat and sleep. He did not mind their ugliness, for somehow that fitted into everything else. But to be scolded through most of the short days of summer and through half of the much longer nights of winter had begun to wear into him, just as a badly sewn seal boot will wear the skin off one's instep.

If he were asked why under these circumstances he continued to shelter this thankless couple, Pituluk could not have told you. It may have been that he had not moral courage to discard them to death, but—much more likely—it was because the law of the North provides that what is enough for one can generally be made sufficient for two, and even for three at a pinch. Also there was the probability that, if he did turn them out, he would meet them later on in the place where there is always plenty of food, and be faced with accusation as well as complaint.

It fell on a hard day when Pituluk returned from a fruitless tramp over leagues of tumbled ice, where the wind drove the drift snow stinging into his face, that his eyes were very hot and sore. At this he was a little anxious, and regained the igloo with nothing but two patches of frost-bite to show for his work. Kugyiyuk waited impatiently when she heard him crawling along the low tunnel. Presently she turned to Tuktu, who was chewing steadily at the last strip of seal-meat.

"Again he has nothing."

Tuktu, to make sure, paused till the hooded head pushed through. He saw that the old woman was right and chewed the faster.

"So many times he comes—and with nothing."

Pituluk cleared the tunnel and, throwing back his hood, put his hand into a stone bowl. This sat over a single spear-head of flame rising from a stone lamp. Dipping up water, he bathed his eyes.

"I saw but one caribou—a coast caribou. It was too far. My eyes are sick. It is the blindness that comes."

Tuktu laughed harshly. "What difference will that make to your hunting?"

Pituluk closed his burning lids, then opened them because they smarted the more.

"Perhaps it will make a difference to you. It is not many months since you have complained and called me a fool. Why then should you care if I stop hunting?"

Tuktu was nearing the end of his strip. "I did not know," he said, with a glance at the spear balanced against the curving wall—"I did not know that you had begun to hunt."

Pituluk did not answer, having just discovered that he could neither open nor close his eyes without hurting himself. He remembered thankfully that he had buried the dogs' harness and stamped it tight in the snow. That was all right. The dogs could get along very well for a few days till his eyes were better.

As for the others, he only chuckled and blinked at the two shapeless forms working into their caribou-skin bags. He would blow out the lamp presently and, placing flint and punk in a safe place, crawl into his own. There he would lie for a while, listening to the drone of cracked voices, while the wind pressed hard on the igloo roof, and far out in Fox Channel the sea ice creaked all night long. He did not rest much. Then, he could not tell at what time, he heard Tuktu speak sharply:

"He sleeps better than he hunts."

Pituluk tried to open his eyes, but the lids were fastened down with a sticky stuff that clung to his fingers when he touched it, and the pain was worse than ever. He felt the two looking at him, and sat up.

"Blindness has come in my sleep."

Kugyiyuk struck fire, lit the lamp, and bent over him. All she could see of Pituluk's eyes were two narrow slits full of something that looked like frozen blubber, only it was soft. She beckoned to Tuktu. "It is true. He is blind."

The hunter moved despairingly. She looked at him again, then got back on to the ledge, where she and the old man whispered, their glistening faces close together. Presently Tuklu also inspected the sick man.

"Water," groaned Pituluk, "bring it to me—I cannot see."

Kugyiyuk slid down. The big man had begun to feel his way across to the stone bowl. She reached ahead of him, and handed it quickly to Tuktu.

"There is no water."

"In the night I was thirsty and drank," quavered her husband. He set the bowl behind him and covered it with a robe.

Pituluk tried to think of the words he once heard a whaling captain use when he was very angry. They struck him at the time as good words, and there was nothing in the Husky language to express what a whaling captain seemed to feel so often. He could not remember them. Nevertheless, he knew there was water in that igloo. A little later, when the two went out, he tried to make fire and melt some for himself. But he only hit his fingers with the flint. He was sorry now that he had not built the igloo out on the ice, even though the wind was worse, because he could have fished through the floor. His grandfather, being also blind, had caught many fish. Then he was more than ever convinced there was water near, and, fumbling about, touched the bowl under the robe. It was already half-frozen, but a good drink still remained. He drained it, put the bowl aside, and groped back. The water lay cold on his stomach, but he felt hot and very angry.

Outside, at a little distance, Tuktu and Kugyiyuk shivered behind a cairn of stones and talked earnestly.

"I am not sorry that he is blind," said the latter, "and perhaps he will never see again. Then we can take what he has and, being rich, will go and live with the tribe at Amadjauk Harbour. It is many years now since Pituluk got angry about that girl and came away."

Tuktu nodded. "When I was in Amadjauk Harbour I saw a box that had a devil in it, and, making sound, talked like a white man. The box is still there, but the devil is asleep and silent. Sulkenulug saw it last summer; I would like to hear that."

She glanced at the igloo, of which the ivory dome was just visible. "You will hear it without doubt. How long can a man live without food?"

"If he be fat, for some time, but if he be cold and thin, not so long. I do not want to see Pituluk die."

"We shall not be there. To-morrow we shall try to kill something, but he must not know if we have meat."

"The smell of a hungry man is sharp," said Tuktu dubiously.

"There will be nothing in the igloo to smell," she grunted.

They went back and found the hunter feeling his spear, running his fingers along its coil of rawhide. Where his eyes used to be were two lines of sticky white.

"I'm hungry," he said dully.

Kugyiyuk's beady gaze rested on his brown, sightless face. She could just see it in the faint flicker of the lamp.

"That is nothing—we are all hungry."

Pituluk's lips lifted. "Do we die here—all of us?"

"Perhaps," put in Tuktu, "we should have starved in any case."

The blind man stumbled to the mouth of the tunnel and stretched himself across it.

"Then we shall die together."

For the next few hours it was very quiet in the igloo. The grey of the sky faded, to be succeeded by a sparkling light of intense cold. Stiffer grew the frost, till the very bones of the hidden earth seemed to shiver and contract. Across the field ice, sharp cannon-like reports zig-zagged out to open water, while the split floes crumpled into irregular ridges of irresistible expansion. The sky, ineffably high and clear, was sown with a host of diamond-pointed lights that became pallid against the curtain of green and yellow flame that hung palpitating in the north. With a low whining, the dogs scratched deeper, till, curled into balls of fur, each lay in his own pit beneath the surface of the driven snow. It was all hard-bitten, bleak and unutterably grim, and only on the far expanse of open sea was there any semblance of life or movement.

Hours later something did move on the ridge behind the igloo, and for a moment a great shape with narrow skull, long lean body and huge flat paws was outlined against the sky. It stood, gaunt and menacing, swaying its white head, gathering into its black nostrils whatever faint odour might be abroad on that crisping night.

A dog stirred in his pit, thrusting a nose into the nipping frost, while the long hair lifted on his spine. For a second he waited thus with every mysterious instinct thrilling in his chilled body. Then the nose lifted higher, and he flung his signal to the moon. Another dog took it up—and another. Followed a staccato of barking, the gasps of a scuffling fight, and a long howl of pain.

Pituluk woke with a start, for the sound of scratching of mighty claws came through the igloo wall. The brute had smelled its window of walrus membrane and, beating off the dogs, was scaling the icy dome.

Tuktu slid down from his shelf, seized the spear, and began to stab weakly upwards. A wide paw crashed through. In the gap, against the twinkling stars, he saw the menacing head and shaggy throat.

"He will break the roof," he panted; "quick—the bow and arrows—very quickly!"

Kugyiyuk snatched them up, trembling, and fitted a shaft to the taut sinew; but there was no strength in her arm. The tough wood defied her.

"Give it to Pituluk," croaked Tuktu.

"Can a blind man fight with a bear?" groaned the latter, not caring much whether he died or not.

"Pull—and I will guide you." Kugyiyuk thrust the weapon into his hands. "Pull! In a minute he will come through."

Pituluk's fingers crooked round the cord.

"Then it will be as you said," he answered grimly, "but I am glad to shoot once again before I die." The arrow-head came back flush with the belly of the bow. A strong man was Pituluk, even in his blindness.

"To the left!" screamed Kugyiyuk. "No, that is too much—now!"

The sinew twanged and simultaneously the great paw was withdrawn. Tuktu could see the savage head twist round, then the bear slithered down, his claws scraping deep grooves in the wall. As he touched the ground there was a storm of frenzied barking, the snap of locking jaws and a deep angry cough. This dwindled gradually till there came silence.

Kugyiyuk breathed hard. "He is gone—we are safe."

Pituluk nodded. "Now we can die quietly."

Next morning, when the world was very dark to the hunter, the two ancient ones went out and laid their fingers in the grooves.

"He was a big bear," said Tuktu regretfully, "and without doubt there was much meat on him."

Kugyiyuk did not answer. She was staring at a dog that lurched toward them, his belly bulging. He licked his long jaws contentedly. Her eyes narrowed.

"There is meat. Come!"

They followed the trail a few hundred yards to higher ground. There they found him, a broken arrow projecting from his throat, flanks and side torn and gaping, a great beast from whose bones half the flesh had been ripped by wild, sharp fangs. It was not only dogs that had feasted there, and the meat could not last much longer.

Tuktu chuckled. "There is enough left for such as us. See, we will not take it into the igloo, but keep it here under the stones. We will eat outside where Pituluk cannot hear us."

They ate as dogs eat, champing the torn flesh with rusty teeth; then, piling rocks on what remained, went back to the igloo.

"Where have you been?" demanded Pituluk suspiciously.

"To look for the bear."

"And you did not find him?"

"Would I not have brought you meat if we had found it?" replied Tuktu.

Pituluk said nothing, but he was aware of a difference he did not understand. Thinking very hard, it seemed that Tuktu's voice was rounder and fuller than before. By now the gnawing in his own stomach was such that he could not sleep. The others, however, did sleep. He whispered to them several times, and got no answer. Also it had struck him that they did not move slowly and painfully any more, like hungry people. They spoke as they always spoke, while he noticed the crack in his own voice. So he lay still for another day.

Then, whispering again to make sure that they slept, he felt his way out through the tunnel. By this time he was very weak, but his eyes did not seem so sticky, and, lifting the lids apart with his fingers, he thought he saw something yellow. Stooping, he found this to be the snow. Winking very hard, the film over his sight lifted a little, and he just made out a narrow trail, tramped deep, that led up the hill. Stumbling along this, he came to a pile of stones.

An hour later, Tuktu sat up suddenly and yawned. "What is it?"

"It is nothing," said the hunter. "I went out to find if I could perhaps see, but everything is black."

Tuktu grinned horribly in the dark. It would not be long now.

Pituluk's voice came in again: "To-morrow let us go to the edge of the ice, where perhaps you can kill a seal."

"It is too rough for a blind man."

"Then you will lead me. It is for the last time, and I will not ask anything more."

Night passed. A block of clear ice had replaced the torn membrane in the roof, and through this there filtered a pale green light in which the hunter could make out two shapeless mounds that snored steadily for hours. As to Kugyiyuk, he did not care much. She was only an old woman, and therefore an old fool with the soul of a fox from which not much could be expected. But with Tuktu it was different. Here was a man who himself had once been a hunter, and was now prepared to look on, his belly full, while another hunter starved. Pituluk didn't think about the ingratitude of it so much as that Tuktu had written himself down as an outcast from the tribes of men.

That was it. An outcast! So Pituluk reached for the spear and re-coiled the rawhide line. The meat in his stomach had thawed, and he experienced sharp pains. But he was glad of them.

About noon, when the sun had mounted to the topmost point of its flat arc, they set out for the edge of the ice. Tuktu went first, then Kugyiyuk, and lastly the hunter, who had stubbornly insisted on carrying the spear and line. "Let him carry it," thought the others. In his left hand he held one end of a thong at which the old woman jerked impatiently. It was a foolish trip, she decided, for one about to die. But as Pituluk peered through the narrow slit between his lids, the snow did not look yellow any longer. It was very familiar, and staring white. Darting swift and unobserved glances, he found that vision had returned. There was still stickiness about his eyes, but he did not wipe it off, and stumbled on, complaining weakly. Presently they came to open water.

"Ah," said Tuktu, "if Pituluk could only see now!"

"What is it?" demanded the hunter.

"A white whale and her calf. There is much meat and they are very close. I would that my arm were not withered, or I could feed you well for many weeks."

But Pituluk had seen. Just against the ice floated a small whale fifteen feet long, the green water surging lazily on its smooth and shining back. It lay languid and was lifted, glistening in the emerald heave of the sea. Beside it pressed a calf, like a fragment detached from the mother floe, while intermittently came the deep and whistling breath that shot a slim and sparkling fountain into the air. "Ah-hoo-nah, ah-hoo-nah," the great fish seemed to sigh, and saw them not.

A thrill ran through Pituluk. "Am I near enough to throw my spear?" he asked unsteadily.

Tuktu smiled coldly. "It matters not. Throw it!"

"How far is the whale?" The hunter's brown fingers closed over the short, straight shaft, and he shook the coiled line so that its loops hung free.

"Half a spear-throw only; but why ask this when you cannot see? Do not hit the mother or you will lose both spear and line when she dives. It is better that I try, and not you."

But Pituluk had raised himself on the balls of his feet and was balanced tensely. Through the slit in his lids the length of the larger whale shone clear and glaring white. He stiffened for the throw, and the anger and contempt and hot hunger for revenge that boiled in him burst forth in a great shout.

"I am very ready to lose them, O Tuktu, with the heart of a wolf! Be thou ready to lose more!"

The shaft streaked forward, and as the point sank through he flipped the swinging coils into the air. They fell neatly over Tuktu's shoulders. The green water swirled violently as the great white body flashed downwards. The whale's ivory shape glimmered for an instant. Then the line tightened, and in a flash Tuktu was snatched forward and twitched into the depths. In another second the tail of the line squirmed over the edge.

Pituluk stared at the bubbles contentedly.

"Let us go back to that pile of stones; I am very hungry."

The white whales still cruise up and down Fox Channel, passing on into Boothia Gulf and the Arctic. From topeck and igloo the small brown people watch them, and when they see beside the larger bulk the shining body of a calf, they chuckle to themselves and say, "It is Tuktu." And when the sparkling jet springs into the light, and the sound of blowing comes across the heaving water, they look at one another.

"Ah-hoo-nah, ah-hoo-nah," they repeat. "It is Tuktu, who asks to be forgiven, down among the salmon."

THE MAGIC OF KAHDOOSH

KAHDOOSH, the Man with a Nose like a Bottle, sat on a flat stone that happened to be on the west coast of Greenland, and stared gloomily at a cluster of topecks huddled on a strip of ground near the shore. The sun was bright and very hot. He scrutinised a pack of mangy dogs hunting for offal along the edge of the sea, saw a group of women go off in the oomiak, or skin boat, screaming with laughter and a great splashing of paddles, and noted with cold and critical gaze that Larpan, the Cross-eyed One, had got into his kayack. He was going to the rocky islands two miles away over the emerald water to determine whether the walrus had yet arrived.

Watching the dipping stroke of double blades that flashed like mirrors in the sun, Kahdoosh felt more than ever a violent antipathy to Larpan. The immediate cause of this was Peegish, the Chatterer, a cylindrical maiden of nineteen years.

Again the eternal triangle. What need to point out that whether in Greenland or Tooting, whether beneath silk or caribou-skin, the human heart aspires with the same longings, throbs with the same profound passion? Tooting may be more voluble than Greenland, but it can harbour no deeper emotions.

The Thames Embankment may be more impressive than the rocky waste in which Peegish was acknowledged to be the leading flapper, but no lover ever leaned on its massive parapet and gazed more moodily at Chelsea Bridge than Kahdoosh now gazed at his particular section of the Arctic Ocean.

The situation had grown acute. It is probable that had the tribe of Kahdoosh lived, say, on the Beaufort Sea, where things are more primitive and old-fashioned, and whaling-ships seldom penetrate, the matter would have been settled months ago in a practical and expeditious manner. But here, in Greenland waters, one was, so to speak, on the fringes of society. It was nothing novel that a Dundee whaler should slide like a ghost into the bay, and drop anchor with a roar of chain that roused the birds for a mile round. Then there were visits on both sides, and as often as not some of the men joined up for the cruise, returning later with wealth, and new rifles, a much enlarged and decorated vocabulary and a general air of superiority that the others sometimes found a trifle irritating.

In the case of Larpan, who had made one such voyage, the trouble was that he then acquired an even more full equipment, having come back nothing short of a full-blown magician. This excited a vast amount of interest and amusement, and the first soirée he gave was in the topeck of Hadjvick, the Man who Lurched when he Walked. Hadjvick was the father of Peegish, and that damsel, with much giggling and flashing of black eyes, was in the front row. Kahdoosh, as not infrequently in such cases, lounged somewhat superciliously at the back against the skin wall.

Larpan began by pulling a red cotton handkerchief from the back of Hadjvick's neck, and accumulated a pile of rabbit's feet from various members of the audience, all of whom disclaimed the possession of such valueless articles. Then he uncovered the skull of a jar seal between the feet of Chantook, the Fat Man, who stared at the thing incredulously amid shouts of laughter. With an insolent glint in his eye, he called up Kahdoosh, and drew from his pocket a metal mirror used exclusively by the women. This made Kahdoosh very hot and angry, for he knew he looked like a fool. Finally, the slant-eyed Peegish herself was summoned, and her well-oiled hair yielded a large collection of walrus-teeth, while that young woman gave a series of little shrieks of admiring surprise, each one of them a dagger in the heart of Kahdoosh. It is true that at the beginning of the performance the figure of Larpan was noticeably bulky, and, later, of merely average girth, but Kahdoosh could not summon courage to call attention to the fact. Magic was magic! The public had no desire to investigate second causes. Without question it was Larpan's night of triumph.

That was a week ago, and Peegish enjoyed the present state of affairs immensely. To be desired by two men, both of prominence in the tribe, meant much to any girl in Greenland. Larpan was a little the older, also not quite as well off as Kahdoosh, but he had unquestionable resources. Also he was better tempered. Kahdoosh, on the other hand, was a great hunter. He did not laugh so much, but in hard times might make a safer partner. Hadjvick pointed out these things, and asked the girl what she was going to do.

"For another six months," he concluded, "I will feed you—but no more. If you have not chosen by then, I will choose for you. I have spoken."

"Which will you choose?" asked Peegish thoughtfully.

He threw a stone at a dog. "There was once a woman of our tribe who, being a fool like all women, married a magician because he did wonderful things. In the middle of the first bad winter it happened that he could not kill anything, and she starved to death. His magic could not get through the fur of a single seal."

Peegish smiled. "Has then a woman no magic of her own?"

"Enough to make wise men at times very foolish, but not enough to make a foolish man wise. The tongue that is always travelling never arrives. As for these two men, it may be that I will give you to the one who makes the greatest magic in six months from now."

"The fingers of Kahdoosh are not long and clever like those of Larpan."

Hadjvick grunted. "Again how like a woman. Is it not the head that directs the fingers? It is well that you tell them both what I say, and in six months we shall see."

Peegish did tell them, with sidelong looks and much digging of a blunt seal-shod foot into the stony soil of Greenland. Then she told everyone in the village. Larpan heard it, smiling, confident and determined to surpass all previous achievements in the way of illusion. Kahdoosh heard it, glum, frowning, with a distant desire for murder in his heart, knowing very well that, practise as he might, he could never bring the skull of a seal out of the ground, or walrus-teeth from a girl's hair. Magic! What had he to do with magic?

All this and a good deal more was in his mind when, sitting on the rock, he observed on the horizon a white speck that he knew to be not a gull's wing but the foresail of a whaler. He watched her grow till the crumpled wave at her stem was visible. She came on into the mouth of the bay and anchored a quarter-mile out. Kahdoosh, staring, remembered that on such a ship as this Larpan had learned his tricks. He wondered if there was any magic on this vessel. Then he saw that Larpan's kayack had altered its course and was headed for the whaler.

Something darted through his brain. He jumped up, dashed bulkily down-hill, and a moment later was driving his own kayack over the smooth water with quick, vicious strokes. He reached the vessel's side at the instant when Larpan caught the tail-end of a rope.

Macgovan, the captain, a hard-bitten sailor who

had killed whales from the Falklands to Spitzbergen, looked keenly at the two. He wanted only one man, and it was difficult to choose. The obvious strength of Kahdoosh was in his favour, but Larpan looked the quicker of them. And both wanted to go. Kahdoosh waited, thinking rapidly. Presently he made a gesture.

"I am a better hunter than Larpan," he said gravely, "but not so great a man."

His rival stared, while Macgovan glanced at him curiously.

"What do you mean?"

"I am only a hunter, but he is a maker of magic."

"Eh?" grunted Macgovan. "What kind of magic?"

"Show him," said Kahdoosh.

Larpan was bursting with pride. What an astonishing tribute, he thought—and at a time like this! Hastily he borrowed a penknife from the cook and a plug of tobacco from the first mate, and brought them both out of Macgovan's ears. The latter perhaps was impressed, but it was hard to say what went on behind a face like his. Larpan rolled his eyes around the grinning circle of the crew, borrowed more articles,and surpassed himself.

"That is nothing," he said modestly; "I can do much more, but it takes time. Much thought have I given to these things."

"It's enough," snapped Macgovan abruptly. "You're no hunter, but a conjuror." He turned to Kahdoosh. "Can you do any of these tricks?"

The big Husky shook his head. "I am not clever enough. I can only hunt."

"Then you're the man for me. Come on board in one hour. Now off with both of you."

The two paddled shoreward without a word. "Not clever enough!" thought Larpan to himself. "Not clever enough!"

Kahdoosh, having no packing to do, used a good deal of that hour talking to Peegish. No details had come out, and for his side of it Larpan would see that they didn't, but it was already known in the village that both men had wanted that job, and Kahdoosh had got it. Peegish learned a good deal more when Kahdoosh asked her to wait, just as they ask in Clapham and Mount Street.

"I go for the whale-hunting," he said earnestly, "and it may be I shall go farther, not coming again till the ice moves in the spring."

Peegish was impressed by the look in his eyes, but there was her father to reckon with.

"Why so long?"

"Because it is in my mind that there is a greater magic than that of Larpan, which deals only with childish things. It is that I seek, and maybe it is not to be found on any whaler. If this be so, then I go to the place where the whaler came from and seek there."

The black eyes surveyed him with sudden respect.

"Perhaps if you did not go you might have me anyway."

Kahdoosh took a long breath. "That is well, but

Larpan found a woman's glass in my pocket, and till I have made him a greater fool than I was then, I shall not be content. If on the other hand you desire this man, why not take him?"

This was a totally new angle for Peegish. To be told in so many words that she might marry Larpan if she wished, and be hanged to her, invested Kahdoosh with an entirely novel interest. No man had ever spoken to her like that before. And since the psychology of the feminine heart is the same on the western coast of Greenland as, say, on the shores of the Mediterranean, she liked him better than ever. Also, she reflected, Larpan would help to pass the time.

"It is well," she said softly, "and I will speak to Hadjvick. It may be that he will feed me till the ice moves."

She told the latter when he was watching the whaler clear the mouth of the bay. He listened, nodded, but never took his eyes from the ship.

"Then let it be till the ice moves," he said dryly. "And it is in my mind that one head is better than many long and clever fingers."

Now of that trip, and the adventures which befell Kahdoosh, it is not necessary to write, such doings being known to many even of those who go not out in ships. There was the grind and hardship and sleet that cut to the bone, and death close at hand many a time. There was the flight of the harpoon, the plunging leviathan, the breathless pursuit with the line tight as a banjo-string over the bow, the death of leviathan, the whaler coming up to the kill like a homing gull, the flenching and rendering—and then the whole thing over again. Kahdoosh liked it all and never complained and, because he felt best when well oiled, was as strong as two horses, had no nerves, and eyes like a cormorant, he found much favour with Macgovan, who knew good stuff when it came his way.

It fell on a morning when the whaler lay becalmed, that Kahdoosh, who lounged amidships, heard voices in the galley—that is the cook was whistling and another singing. This was very strange, as the former seemed to be alone. Presently he came out, spat over the rail and passed the time of day. The voice, however, continued. It was something like Macgovan's. Kahdoosh stared, and when the cook went forward he peered in through the galley window. No one there! Still the voice! At this his stomach rolled over inside him.

The cook, returning, found him gripping the rail, his whole body stiff.

"What's the matter wi' ye, Dooshy?"

"Many things. There is a devil on this ship."

"What are ye talkin' about, ye big loon?"

Kahdoosh held up a warning hand. "Listen!"

From the galley drifted the voice: "I lo'e a lassie, a bonnie Hielan' lassie."

"What is it that speaks without a mouth? No man is there. Is this magic?"

Cookie grinned, hooked his arm and steered him, unwilling, to the galley door.

"It's naethin' but a bit box that the sound comes out of. Look under yon table."

Kahdoosh looked very hard, and his lips felt dry. The box wasn't much bigger than his head. Something in it was going round and round. This stopped with the noise that a dog makes when he scratches the ice. The voice ceased.

"The devil is dead," he said thickly.

"Aye, that one. Now we'll try another."

For the next quarter-hour cookie enjoyed the study of the pagan face, while the black eyes never blinked and marvellous thoughts darted rapidly through that savage brain. Undoubtedly great magic, this! Greater by far than Larpan ever dreamed of.

"The words," he said slowly, "how is it there are words without a tongue and throat? Where do they come from?"

Cookie held up a record. "They're on this, ye auld pagan."

"Who put them on?"

"I dinna ken."

"But how did he put them?"

"Simple enough. There's a place where they're made, and if ye talk on to the thing it talks back."

"Like a woman?"

"Aye, verra like a woman."

"Where is this place?"

Cookie indicated the eastern horizon. "Over yonder, where we come from."

"Will it give back any kind of words, or is it they must be those of a white man?"

"Any kind."

"Then this devil does not care what he says?"

"Not a hoot."

Kahdoosh pulled down his brows because the intensity of his thoughts hurt him.

"Does the ship go to that place?"

"Aye—or near it."

"Then I go with the ship. Let the devil now sleep a little."

Of the rest of that voyage it is written that, when he was not flenching or rendering or pulling stroke oar in the whaling-gig, Kahdoosh spent his time with the devil, over whom he soon gained a complete control. He made a picture when his big, strong hand fitted a needle, and he learned to finger a record as lightly as one would a bubble. His wages loomed very large in his mind during these days, and when he heard from Macgovan that he would have more than enough to buy a large strong devil with many voices, his cup was full. Now, too, he watched the white man more closely than ever before, picking up more and more English till, at the end of an extended voyage, when he set foot in Dundee and arrayed himself in Scotch tweeds, he was a very different Husky from the one who sat on a flat rock and tortured his soul with thoughts of Peegish and Larpan. Larpan—the son of many fools! But he wanted Peegish more than ever.

It fell on a day when the water was running down a thousand streams of Greenland that Macgovan's whaler rounded a point on the western coast and headed for an anchorage well known to her master. In the bow stood Kahdoosh, garbed as no Husky had been garbed before in that desolate region. His boots hurt a good deal, but the vivid pattern of his tweeds made up for that. He stood motionless, picking out the topeck of Hadjvick, which was pitched in the same place, and marking diminutive figures that grew slowly larger. No—it was nothing like Dundee or the other ports where he had worked all winter. But it was home—home with the rocks and jar seals and mangy dogs and kayacks dancing on the water—and Peegish. The seed of the North was too deep-rooted in his pagan breast to be destroyed by anything he had seen or done. Thus does the cold hand of the Arctic claim her own.

Peegish was there when he landed in the middle of an awed circle with great good-humour and two large bundles. She had indeed been fed by her father till the ice moved, but not without protest, since her appetite was hearty. Now she stared at her lover with uncontrollable excitement, and got just one look. That was enough. Larpan, who had developed several new tricks that greatly enhanced his reputation, was also there, a little contemptuous about the Scotch tweeds, but vastly curious as to the bundles. More magic, no doubt—but he felt safe enough. Hadjvick, congratulating himself that his larder was now to be relieved of a strain, reckoned that the trousers of Kahdoosh would make admirable lampwick, and decided if the wanderer gained the day to put that price on the hand of his daughter.

Then there were the rest of them, hunters, women and children, all talking at once, fingering the fringe of the strange clothing, the men trying not to show how jealous they were, the women prodigiously impressed, the children staring with round black eyes. It was a great home-coming.

Followed a little silence, till Kahdoosh dropped into the Husky tongue as smoothly as oil flows into a bottle. He looked at Larpan out of the corner of his eye while he spoke.

"It is known to all that between me and Larpan there is a matter to be settled. It is well that it be settled now, and for this purpose I have come back. But to make that which I will make, it is necessary that I be alone first. Who then will lend me his igloo for the space of a short time?"

"I will," said Hadjvick promptly. His was the biggest of all.

Kahdoosh nodded. "It is well."

He picked up his bundles, stalked to the home of Peegish, and retired to solitude. The village waited expectant. Larpan felt a little nervous, admitting that this was a good opening and contributed the desirable touch of mystery. He did a few tricks in the sight of everybody just to show that he didn't care, but they were old and missed fire. What was Kahdoosh up to? That was the question. Presently the latter appeared and waved a hand. The village trooped in, silent, wondering. The topeck was exactly as before. Nothing touched or altered. Peegish squatted in the front row, with Larpan lounging this time against the back wall. The semicircle formed—black brows—narrow, slanting eyes—rows of copper-coloured faces—teeth that glittered—oily hair that fell to the strong shoulders. Kahdoosh took it all in and nodded gravely.

"It is now nearly a year since I went away," he began, "and many strange things have I seen in the land where the whaling-ships rest in winter. There are igloos like sand on the shore, built of stone both red and white, and many devils are slaves of the people. Being too impatient to walk, they journey in things like an oomiak which has a roof and runs along the ground more quickly than a coast caribou. There is fire for all, made of stones that come out of the earth, and water runs where they will in long tubes like a bear's entrails. Plenty of meat there is, also a white food made of a certain powder, which is burned with fire and goes into the stomachs of all. In the night-time they have light in small bottles wherein are certain devils who shine very brightly when there is need of them. But the greatest devil of all is one who runs like lightning with a great roaring, following a certain path prepared for him, and pulling behind him more people than there are in many villages."

"Ey-yah," said Hadjvick, "what wonders are these? Is Kahdoosh then talking of what he dreamed?"

"No," smiled the traveller, "but only of that which I saw and also touched. But of all these devils the most strange is the one who takes to himself the voice of those dead or distant, and speaks for them."

This was too much. Larpan began to laugh, while even the faith of Peegish tottered. Kahdoosh did not change a muscle.

"It is truth that I tell, and furthermore it is the law that this devil, being very wise, also speaks only the truth. That which he says is believed of all men, and when his word goes forth there is none that answers back. He has a tongue, but no ears; and having no head yet remembers many things. That devil has come here with me. Even now he is in this topeck."

A shiver ran through the audience. They glanced fearfully about. Nothing visible here—no devil—only the utensils of Hadjvick—a pile of greasy skins—two stone lamps and some gear. Kahdoosh marked the shiver and lifted the door-flap.

"What remains to be said is outside. Sit you close there."

They filed out, squatting within a few feet of the opening. He stepped back, and the flap closed. A little silence. Then came a sort of throaty chant, the voice of Kahdoosh.

"I, the devil of all truth, tell of Larpan, who, being in no manner a hunter, but desiring a certain woman, learned for himself some tricks to make his name great in his village. This man, filling his sleeves with walrus-teeth . . ."

Here the audience sat up very straight, for Kahdoosh still telling his story came out, dropped the flap and sat in the midst of them. But, wonder of wonders, the voice went on inside.

". . . filling his sleeves with walrus-teeth, and burying the skull of a jar seal in the ground, brought forth these things, pretending that"—here Peegish screamed and Larpan's eyes bulged—"that he was a magician. Fools there were in the village that believed him, so he sat up with his fingers at night, making them smooth for more tricks. But because his mind was empty like a pool in which there are no fish, and his head soft like a child's, and his arm weak like that of an old woman, it came that the tribe grew weary of his foolishness, and the woman he desired laughed in his face and married another."

With that the voice ceased, making a little noise like a dog does when it scratches the ice.

"Ou-uh!" breathed the audience. "Ou-uh!" Here indeed was magic surpassing the wildest dream. They looked at Larpan for his answer.

He got up shakily, glared at Kahdoosh, seemed about to speak, then marching stolidly to his own topeck went in and drew the flap tight.

The village watched him without words, but the father of Peegish wasted no thought on Larpan. He leaned over and spoke into the hollow of his daughter's ear:

"If the trousers of your husband please you not, I am in great need of lamp-wick."

THE REWARD OF KWASIND

KWASIND, whose name in English means the Strong Man, lived with his daughter Suggemah, the Mosquito, in a conical teepee on the iron-bound shores of Lac Seul, which lies roughly half-way between Lake Superior and Hudson Bay. Should you desire to know more of Lac Seul, it will suffice to say that the surrounding country is flat and rocky, the timber small and straggling, the fishing good, the fur better than good, the summers are hot and sweltering, the winters bleak and smitten with biting winds.

This is one of the many regions of the North once administered by the factors of the Company of Gentlemen Adventurers who became in time lords of the territory they penetrated, and developed into the undisputed rulers of the Land of Little Sticks, till later their sway was challenged by others; but Kwasind, being a conservative by nature, preferred to do business at the old shop. Also there was the fact that Mactavish, the nearby factor, was a man of few words, who had the habit of doing rather better than his promise. And that helped trade a great deal.

It fell, during a winter when the winds were unusually bitter, that there passed through the Lac

Seul country the story that white men were looking through spy-glasses that stood on three legs to ascertain if there could be found a good trail for the thing that vomited fire, and ran on wheels, and carried many, many men in its entrails. Kwasind, like other Ojibways in the district, heard this story, and hoped greatly that there was nothing in it. For one thing, there were enough white men as matters stood. For another, any such arrangement would certainly affect the hunting and trapping. He understood a little English, but had small respect for the men he learned it from, excepting always Mactavish. And, after all, it was his country, and not theirs.

He was thinking about this one day while going the round of his traps, which meant a circuit of about a hundred and thirty miles, and took about a week, when he noticed that a recent snowshoe-trail cut across his old one, a trail that had certainly been made within the last few hours. Also he saw in a moment that it was a white man's trail, that the man was tired or sick, about six feet tall, limped a trifle on his left leg, was not sure where he was going, and carried a pack that was but loosely strapped to his shoulders.

There were a good many other points about the trail that one could not mistake—for instance, that the shoes had been made by old Keego, on Manitou Lake, that the man had one very sore heel, and some of the fingers of his left hand were frozen. These were of minor interest. The one that stood out was that the stranger needed help, and needed it badly.

He found the man in less than half a mile, found him in a tumbled heap, with his eyes shut, and grey patches on his cheeks; whereupon Kwasind got very busy, and in six minutes was holding a cup of steaming tea to the stiff lips. In sixteen minutes he was smashing down the trail to his nearest hunting-shack, grunting words of encouragement over his doubly-burdened shoulder to the figure that staggered behind him. Twenty-four hours later he lifted the flap of the teepee on Lac Seul and motioned the stranger in. The latter obeyed, swayed weakly for an instant, then pitched forward on his face.

Now, it is written—though few there be that are wise enough to read before the punishment comes for disobedience—that the wilderness has rules of her own. To follow these without question is to be safe. To violate them is to invite the inevitable. Young Murchison, who in nature and mind could not be called a thoroughbred, and was late from the office of an engineering firm that did their business in the sober purlieus of Victoria Street, S.W., had not read the rules, and thereby committed certain grievous errors. He left camp not very sure of where he was going, he started out tired and with a sore heel, in the first half-hour he lost the mitt from his left hand, and, lastly, did not trouble to watch the sun, of which there may be but little in such regions in winter, nor did he bother to adjust his pack, which, swinging loosely, added to his fatigue without his knowing it. Also a bit of shrapnel near his left knee had begun to burn like fire. So, taking one thing with another, the conclusions of Kwasind might be considered fairly accurate.

Twelve hours later the white man stretched his six-foot length of weary body—Kwasind had estimated his height by the length of his stride—and opened his eyes. His feet were swollen, and the patches on his cheeks very tender. He was lying beside a smokeless fire of dry wood, from which vagrant sparks danced upward to an opening where the teepee poles met and crossed. The camp was floored with balsam-boughs, over which lay caribou robes and rabbit-skin blankets, the latter made of long one-inch-wide strips woven into a sort of loose fabric. On the other side of the fire sat Suggemah, her black hair in two long thick braids that trailed over her supple shoulders. She was very busy with something, and presently Murchison made out that she was mending a pair of moccasins. They looked like his own. He studied the smooth, impassive face, the high cheek-bones, the squareness of her small, strong wrists, the quick certainty of the slim, brown hands. Then he met a glance from her black eyes. It was queer, he thought, to be alone with a heathen girl like this. And where was the man?

"Hungry?" asked Suggemah. She had been practising her English for hours past, repeating it over in whispers to herself, and greatly intrigued with the whole situation.

"Very hungry," he replied, feeling that he could have gnawed contentedly at the blanket that covered him.

She made a soft little noise in her throat, and lifted the lid from a pot by the fire. Instantly the teepee was filled with the most seductive odours. There was a partridge in that pot, and a bit of bacon—which on Lac Seul was worth a dollar and a half that winter, or, say, the price of a fairly prime mink-skin—and a lump of caribou meat, half a whitefish that Kwasind had lifted from beneath the ice a few hours previously, and some balls of flour, known in the North as doughboys, which provide what may be called the cementing agent to every really solid meal. All these had been simmering in a slow, deliberate fashion that permitted none of their virtues to escape, and now sent out an invitation that made Murchison lick his swollen lips and stretch an eager hand.

"Not much first time," said Suggemah, smiling gravely. "Eat more by and by. White man make much sick eat too much."

He ate slowly, which was an effort, watching her out of the corner of his eye. There was a good deal of the aristocrat about her. She didn't stare at him, or giggle, or do any of the things that some girls he knew would have done in the circumstances, nor was she in any way self-conscious. The teepee was clean and tidy, her clothes—which she had evidently made herself—were neat and well finished, and there was that in her face and manner which said very plainly that she expected to be treated by this stranger with exactly the consideration she had for him. This was her party, and in her father's house.

Presently he put down an empty dish with an eloquent sigh. "That was very, very good. No more now?"

"Smoke!" said Suggemah, and handed him his own pipe. "My father come back soon. Me make your feet better now."

She rubbed them with an ointment of herbs and bear's grease that soothed the fire in his flesh, and there seemed to be healing in her very touch. He was smoking thoughtfully, wondering how to thank her, when from close by in the bush came a sudden squealing cry that sounded strangling and almost human. He looked at her, startled.

"Me snare wahboose-rabbit. Plenty wahboose this this winter. Last winter not many. Every seven years great sickness kill them."

"Where is your father?"

"He go see traps. You go sleep now. He here when you wake up."

Murchison did as he was bid, it being very easy to obey. He dreamed as he slept, with visions of other Samaritans of whom he had read, especially of One, grave and tender, while into his dreams drifted the dull reports from the bleak expanse of Lac Seul where the ice expanded and heaved in the intense frost, and a lone timber wolf howled hungrily from the slope of a distant ridge. And all the time, hour after hour, Suggemah tended the fire, lest the stranger be cold, replenishing its blaze from the pile of wood at the teepee door.

There were many questions she wanted to ask

when he woke, but her English could not go that far. What did girls of her own age do and look like in the land he came from? Was the trapping good, and were there plenty of rabbits? What did one pay for a red flannel skirt at the trading-posts? Was the snow deep in winter, and the birch-bark good for canoe-making? And when a girl married, did she have to work very hard, and chop wood, and feed the dogs, and pull the nets from under the ice? That was the job Suggemah liked least, though she had never dreamed of saying so.

All these things would fall to her lot, and because she rather dreaded them she was staying with her grave, kindly father as long as she possibly could. But there was no escape from Fate.

Late that night Murchison heard the yelp of dogs a mile away, and presently the creak of shoes outside the teepee, then the stamp of feet, and Kwasind came in, a tall, white pillar of a man with frost rime sparkling on his upper lip. He glanced at his guest, nodded to Suggemah, and said not a word till he had eaten.

"Me go your camp tell everybody you all right come back to-morrow," he remarked presently. "Everybody think you big fool get lost and die."

Murchison thought that this bordered on the personal. But he probably had been a fool of some description. So he merely tried to explain that he knew nothing of the North, which was quite unnecessary, and that he was one of a survey party exploring for a new railway.

Kwasind nodded. "Why you make railway here?"

"To open up the country and bring lots of people." The young man said this with a touch of pride, and saw himself waving the banner of progress.

The Indian made a deliberate gesture, fingers out, palm down.

"Plenty people here now. Me no want your fire-wagon. This my country. You keep fire-wagon at home your country. Great Spirit tell me last night fire-wagon no good for Land of Little Sticks. Frighten mink and otter and caribou. Big noise and much stink."

Murchison felt amused and rather patronising. Without doubt he was dealing with a very limited intelligence, and Kwasind did not mean to be rude, nor did he realise that he would make money more easily after the railway was built, and would benefit in many ways at present past the comprehension of a benighted heathen.

"That's all right," he said carelessly, "and you'll soon get used to it."

It was a social and tactical error. What Murchison had failed to perceive was that for the time being he was the guest of a member of one of the oldest aristocracies in the world, a man who was proud to a degree that only a very few understand, a man who had been weighing him with remarkable care. Kwasind was very wise in some ways, and very ignorant in others, but he knew much, and was therefore very far from being a fool. He understood the instincts of animals, and the ways of fur and feather, and could read the skies like an open book, and was brave and simple and honest, and could and did live well where a white man would starve. As to white men in general, his experience told him that his people were usually better off without them, excepting always the Hudson Bay factors, who often married Indians, that union producing the best all-round specimen to be found in the woods—the Scotch half-breed.

And Kwasind did want the country for his tribe and himself. It wasn't much to ask, and the fur not as good as it used to be, and what he could not understand was why men should leave their own territory to invade his. As for a railway, he had the feeling that it would be the beginning of the end.

"Suppose me make fire-wagon pass close by your teepee, you no like him, eh?" he said after a long pause.

"I'd rather like it," chuckled Murchison, "and if I didn't I'd move the teepee. That's what you'll have to do, old man."

Kwasind said nothing, having made up his mind to that long ago, and presently his guest noted the beauty of the soapstone pipe around which the strong brown fingers curved so contentedly.

"I say, what will you take for that pipe?"

Kwasind regarded him calmly. That pipe had been smoked by his great-grandfather all the way from Lake Superior to the Coppermine River. It was saturated with tradition and history, a thing beyond purchase, consecrated by the vanished lips that once closed over its stem, the companion of lonely hours when the winds were bitter, the solace for punishing days when one tightened the leather thong round one's empty stomach. Such things were not sold.

But the longer Murchison stared, the more he coveted. It was utterly unlike any pipe he had ever seen, with the wing-bone of a crane for a stem, and he ached to take it back to London, show it to admiring friends, and tell them of his adventure on Lac Seul while he filled it with British tobacco, not the filthy stuff that the present owner seemed to fancy.

"I'll give you five dollars."

Kwasind shook his head.

"Ten!"

Ten dollars was the price of seven prime mink-skins on Lac Seul that winter, and a deal of money, but Kwasind did not give a sign.

"Fifteen!" said Murchison. "Better let me have it. You can make another any day."

Kwasind took the pipe from his mouth, looked at it fixedly, and held it out. There was an expression in his eyes that his guest only understood later on.

"Take it!"

Murchison's hand was in his pocket, when Kwasind added with a curious inflexion: "Keep it. I do not sell, but give."

It was very silent in the teepee that night, with not even a whine from the dogs half-buried in the snow outside, and the white man, in a rabbit-skin sleeping-bag, lay on his back and thought for a long time. He rather felt he had put his foot in it. Kwasind had not said another word, nor had Suggemah, on the subject of the pipe, so the only thing to do was to settle up next morning in so liberal a fashion as to wipe out any sense of loss the gift might have occasioned. If he gave the old fellow twenty-five dollars for saving his life, that ought to put everything straight. And Suggemah could get no end of an outfit with twenty-five dollars.

At noon on the following day he stood on the summit of a ridge, and Kwasind pointed to a pencil of grey smoke that rose from a clump of dark-green spruce far below. They had come to it as a bird flies across country, and on the way Kwasind indicated the run of the water, the slope of the hills, the boundaries of lakes, and numberless other things of infinite value to an engineer. It gave him no pleasure to do this, but it was his duty as a host, even though it made the advent of the fire-wagon all the more certain. Then, with the stranger's camp in sight, and the stranger himself safe and restored, he said a grave good-bye.

Murchison put out his hand. "Here's twenty-five dollars, and thank you."

Kwasind drew himself up to his full height and waved aside the money. His dark, smooth face was stern, and he gave a smile that the young man thought was almost contemptuous.

"No take money for help sick man. Some day, perhaps, you do same for me."

In the next moment Murchison was alone. His host

had vanished like a spirit over the crown of the ridge, and there was left only his fresh trail, with the snow crumbling in over the edges, and the dull sound of an axe, softened as it rose from the adjoining valley.

. . . . .

Some two years later there stood on the stage of a London hall a group of Indians with painted faces and variegated garments of gaudy colours. Their narrow, black, unwinking eyes took in the serried rows of the audience, the staring lights, and the great dome of the building that housed them. To their ears came the murmur of a multitude, and they caught a strange odour that rose from packed humanity. They did not know what to think, for this, and all that had preceded it, was too far removed from anything they had known before. But they were aware that they were there to be stared at. At home they did not paint their faces, nor attire themselves in scarlet and yellow and emerald green. That was left for the young squaws, who, naturally, were fools. But the interpreter had explained that the white people expected it, and it was all covered in the contract which the Indian agent had read over very carefully before he allowed Kwasind to make his cross at the bottom. The money had been paid in advance, and waited his return to Lac Seul with Suggemah.

All this was arranged after a white man had made in the North the picture which had been shown them the day they reached London. It was very great magic. Kwasind was in it, and Suggemah, and even old Keego, for whom a messenger had been sent to Manitou Lake, because he had a face like an owl with its beak chopped off. They had all fished and hunted, and done the things they did, anyway, while the white man said strange words through the interpreter, and twisted at a thing on three legs that had a large glass eye and made a noise like a woodpecker against a hollow log. They had journeyed in the entrails of the fire-wagon, in fire-canoes that had many bowels, one on top of the other; they had crossed a great lake of bitter water, where all the islands had been washed away, and an evil spirit turned their stomachs upside down within them, and the chief of the fire-canoes worshipped the sun every day at noon, raising his arms to heaven in the middle of his prayer. And now, at the end of it all, there were white people like the leaves in summer, and a great noise and many strange smells.

Kwasind and Suggemah were sick of the whole thing. They didn't mind being stared at, but they hated to sleep in small rooms in a large place where there was no air. One could not trap or hunt here, and when one night Kwasind stole out by himself and snared a rabbit in a little clearing where there were trees, and many people rowed themselves in boats in the daytime, there was much trouble, and many words by men who wore blue clothes. He had snared a duck, too, while it slept, and had it under his clothes all the time, but felt it was wiser to say nothing about it. As to Suggemah, she was tired, and bewildered at things she did not understand, and a little jealous because she could never look like the women she saw. So between the two there was a deep longing for the expanse of Lac Seul, and to meet someone who knew their own country, and would talk to them, even if not in their own tongue, about the simple things they knew and missed and loved so greatly.

One night, when this hunger lay heavy on the heart of Kwasind, and he was more than usually sick of his green blanket and the paint on his cheeks, he happened to pick out amongst the blur of the audience one face that he actually knew. It was that of the man whose life he had saved. He had wondered for a while if he would see Murchison, but that possibility was put aside. Now the extraordinary thing had actually happened. He whispered it to Suggemah, and she too stared hard. Then she nodded.

"It is the same man," she said under her breath.

"There is much that I would say to him," murmured her father, "and he has a debt to pay. No doubt he will take me for a while out of this place to where there is wood and water, and the wind blows, and I can snare something. I would speak to him now in the sign language, but he would not understand. What shall I do?" He paused, feeling very helpless. "There is not any trouble in finding a man in the woods, but here is one that I see, yet cannot reach."

Suggemah thought quickly. "Without doubt he

will go away by the big door wherein he came, so if we were there first it would be easy. When the magic has nearly moved across the wall, tell the interpreter that your stomach is sick within you, and go to the big door and wait. When he comes out, tell the young man what is in your heart, and without doubt he will be very glad."

Kwasind nodded, and did as was arranged. So it happened that for a quarter-hour he stood like a graven image at the big door, with the flaring lights of a London street full on his painted face. His arms were folded, and not a muscle of him stirred. His dark eyes, lustrous and steady, betrayed nothing, but his heart was full of a great hunger. In all these millions there was not one he knew amongst the white men, saving only the man he waited for. He saw again the half-frozen figure beside the unsteady trail, remembered Murchison's gratitude when he said good-bye, felt again the smooth surface of the soapstone pipe he had prized so greatly and given so quietly, and reckoned that now, at any rate, the white man would find some suitable way of saying "Thank you!" in his own fashion. Moments passed. People glanced at him, remarked smilingly that it was good advertising, and passed on. Then came the sound of many feet.

Kwasind's eye flashed and his body stiffened. The avalanche surged by, growing in volume, and he surveyed it with a gaze keener by far than any he met. Girls stared at him, nudged each other, and giggled. Men regarded him, closer now than before, and nodded understandingly. He saw all of them—and none. Suddenly he stepped forward, put out an arm like an iron bar, and touched someone on the shoulder.

"Boozhoo!" he said huskily. "Boozhoo! You remember Lac Seul?"

Murchison pulled up, peered hard into the strong face, noble in spite of its fantastic colouring, and gave a quick laugh of delighted recognition.

"By all the Powers! Were you on that platform?"

"Yes," said Kwasind. "Me there, and see you."

Murchison blinked, shouldered his way to the edge of the crowd, and looked at this friend who had suddenly appeared, an older and wiser Murchison, with a good many of his corners knocked off by work and experience. In the past two years he had thought a good deal about Lac Seul, and now saw himself in a not very favourable light so far as that incident was concerned. But one couldn't undo it. Queer how at this moment the sight of Kwasind should revive the chill of frost in his body, and make him feel again the numbing approach of that stupor from which no man awakes in the North. He was aware of this, and a good deal more.

"Suggemah," he asked, "is she here, too?"

The father of Suggemah nodded.

"Good! Where do you live?"

Kwasind made a gesture that embraced North London.

"Will you and Suggemah come and see me now? I want to talk about Lac Seul."

Kwasind's heart leapt, but not a muscle of his face moved.

"You wait. Me get her."

What happened in the next hour always remained in the mind of the hunter as the sort of thing one liked to remember. He and Suggemah embarked in one of the smaller stink devil-wagons that ran about the streets, and came to a big teepee in a row of teepees all made of stone. There the white man brought them to a room wherein sat an old woman of his own tribe, and told her that these were the friends from Lac Seul of whom he had often spoken. Thereupon the woman kissed Suggemah on both cheeks, and held Kwasind's hands for some time, making a queer noise like a laugh, but with tears on her cheeks—which surely was a strange thing. After that was much feasting on many kinds of food brought by another white woman, who screamed as though in fear the first time she entered the room. Then talk of Lac Seul, and much smoke. In the middle of the smoke the young man slapped his leg as though bitten by many mosquitoes at once, and, going away, came back, smiling, with the soapstone puagun, or pipe, at the sight of which, as Kwasind put it, his stomach rolled over and he desired it greatly. Five—ten—fifteen—twenty-five dollars—he was a man of substance and could afford to buy it now. The longer he looked, the greater became his desire. But it had been his gift, so he said not a word.

For a moment Murchison did not say anything

either, but stood with the ancient thing in his fingers, glancing oddly from the hunter to his mother. Very deliberately he filled it and struck a match. Kwasind quivered ever so slightly, his beady eyes fixed on the treasure of his tribe.

"Was this a peace pipe?" asked Murchison.

"Sometimes a peace pipe. It has seen both peace and war."

"But it was never a pipe of reproach?"

Kwasind's dark brows wrinkled a little.

"I do not know that word."

Murchison reddened, glanced at his mother, then took one puff, and held out the puagun to its rightful owner.

"I believe that," he said, "but I do. Here you are, old chap!"

THE LOYALTY OF PEEGUK

PEEGUK, the Flat-footed One, lived, when he was at home, not a thousand miles from Fort Herschell, and, for the Arctic, this is a fairly close address, from which he would be easily found by one who knew the country. Fort Herschell is, as all the world knows, a mass of rock as big as two or three English counties, and situated not a great way from the mouth of the Coppermine River. It is wind-whipped, storm-smitten and ice-blistered, and, in the short-lived summer, occasionally quite warm. The fort—though there is no fort—is the farthest north spot where abide the representatives of law and order.

Peeguk's very mobile headquarters were on the mainland. Sometimes he found it rather lonely, and this in spite of the fact that his joys and sorrows were shared by Oomgah, the Moon-faced One. There was never any shortage of food. White whales, for instance, came ashore every now and then in summer, and as soon as Peeguk saw that they were firmly wedged among the rocks he would move his topeck—or, rather, Oomgah moved it—to the nearest point, and the whale furnished a free lunch counter from which, perhaps for weeks, they carved lean and fat as their leisurely fancy desired. By night the white bears slouched up to help themselves, and after them the lesser fry of the curved-clawed, short-furred, sharp-toothed family; so under this combined assault the whale, which only weighed from twelve to fifteen tons, did not last very long. But it was all quite amicable, with the rules of precedence mutually remembered and recognised.

It happened on a day that some coast Huskies came along in the fine weather, floating like gulls on the placid sea, and camped at the mouth of Wind River, not far from the summer residence of Peeguk. Amongst them was a certain Atokwok, the Far-sighted One, known to many of the small brown tribes as being wise and of great experience. Especially was he learned when it was a matter of the doings and habits of white men. And it occurred when Peeguk and he were sharing a still living salmon that the latter had just jerked up through six fathom of cold green water, that Peeguk, whose throat was full of fish, asked if there was anything new in that particular part of the world.

Atokwok picked a salmon-bone out of his gums and waved a greasy hand.

"I have come from the island on a whaler to the mouth of the Mother of Rivers" (he meant the Coppermine) "and thence here. But on the island I saw those who had arrived from the far south, bringing with them a strange new devil. Never before have I beheld such a devil."

"Does it live in a box, and speak without a tongue, and make a noise like a dog scratching the ice when its speech is finished?"

Atokwok shook his head. "No—not that one—but nevertheless kindred to it, for, of a truth, this I saw is born in a box. But it will not stay there, and leaps out of it across a place as big as many topecks, whereupon it sticks to the wall."

Peeguk blinked at him. "Then you can catch it, or scrape it off?"

"Not so: for when I tried to do this there was much laughter, and my hand went through the devil and felt only the wall."

"Then it escaped—for there cannot be a devil made out of nothing."

"Yet there is, and I who speak to you have seen it. It is the spirit of a very powerful and active one, and lives in the dark."

"Since when has my brother seen in the dark?" asked Peeguk satirically.

Atokwok, undisturbed, and looking very superior, helped himself to the tail of the salmon.

"Verily this thing crossed the dark on a bridge of light, as the ice makes a bridge over a narrow lane of deep water in a season of the year. Thus it came to the wall of which I spoke, and there it stuck."

Peeguk surveyed his visitor gravely. Men did not lie to each other when they sat on a flat rock, side by side, and ate fish on the shore of the sea. At least Eskimo men did not. But all this was a deal harder to swallow than the salmon. A devil that stuck to a wall, and could not be scraped off! Then he had an idea.

"Had it a voice?"

"No—nor was there any sound save a small rattling noise in the box from which it jumped. But no voice."

"And your hand went through it, touching the wall?"

"As I have told you. The part I touched was water, with many strange boats on it, boats that moved with men in them, speaking, it seemed, together; and though I dipped my hand in this water I felt no cold nor was my hand even wet. Have you no more salmon?"

Peeguk did not answer at once, being too occupied with many reflections, novel and stirring. He knew enough to realise that the white man was all-powerful. It was always a surprise to him to hear that a white man had died, and attributed it to the fact that one of the numerous devils in their service had for a moment got the better of his master—which was not infrequently correct. In a way it made one feel more contented with one's own lot. This last revelation, however, surpassed anything he had ever heard.

"No," he said slowly, "but in the next bay is what is left of a young whale whose meat is rotten and therefore very tender. What size is this devil of which you speak?"

Atokwok heaved himself up. "How far away is that whale?"

"As far as a tired man can walk in one hour." He put it this way because all men who are tired cover about the same distance in a given time. "Again I ask how large is this devil?"

"Twice as long as my arms can reach, and twice as high; and," added Atokwok impressively, "it all came out of a hole in the box of a bigness that could be filled by the nose of a jar seal."

He waddled off, his own nose questingly in the air, for thereby he would inevitably find what he sought, and Peeguk sat quite motionless. He gave up trying to understand, but at that moment there was born in him the determination to see this thing for himself. If Atokwok was a liar—well, the word would go forth to that effect; and if he was not—well, the heart of the hunter swelled at the very thought. So because he wanted to work the thing out carefully in his own mind, he asked no more questions, and when Atokwok and his friends moved off eastward next morning into the empty wastes of the Beaufort Sea, Peeguk merely waved a hand and said nothing. But the kayacks of the voyagers had hardly vanished round the nearest point when he turned to Oomgah with an odd look in his oily black eyes.

"I go to see something of which Atokwok has told me, and in two months I shall be at the mouth of the Mother of Rivers. Meet me there with the dogs."

That was all he said, this being a matter he had decided to handle himself, and he went off with the quiet assurance of those who can live without fire or water, and whose larder is the deep green sea from which they take what they need when they need it. He did not worry about Oomgah, she being well able to take care of herself in this fat season of the year, when the salmon lay like silver slabs in the shallow waters, and the runways beside the small inland lakes were crowded with plump, pink-fleshed, half-feathered geese and swans that waddled coastwards while their plumage grew. Nor did storms delay Peeguk, and day after day his kayack, tight as a drum and unsinkable as a soda-water bottle, nosed along the naked shores of the Arctic, its slim prow set steadfastly toward Herschell Island. Then, for the last leg of the trip, an obliging Alaskan whaler gave him a lift over from the mainland, during which he worked his passage with rising excitement in his barrel-like breast.

He approached the fort with strange misgivings that intensified when he learned from a Coppermine Husky of the notable things which were being done there almost every night. It was certainly great magic. The man who told him this said, his eyes rolling, that once he had crept up to a window of the fort, and, looking in, beheld two white men fighting with guns against the wall, that one of them was killed—for he fell down and did not move, and there was no noise at all of fighting or firearms.

"This thing I saw," he repeated earnestly, "so, being much afraid, I ran away, and for two days watched the fort from a little distance. But there was no white man's body carried out to be put with those who died of the great sickness, nor was there any sadness or mourning. Without doubt it is a place of devils, many and strong, and there lies much danger in this matter."

"Why?" demanded Peeguk, setting his teeth.

"It is in my mind that when a man is thus killed, he is forthwith eaten. Otherwise where is his body?"

Peeguk took a long, long breath. In the year of the great hunger men had been eaten on the shore of the Beaufort Sea, and he knew it. But they were mostly old men—who could be spared, and an old woman or two—not of much value. This, however, was spoken of only in whispers, because evil things had befallen many of those who thus saved themselves. Pitalik, for instance, who ate some of his grandfather, was killed by a bear within two months; and Sinuluk, the Large-eared One, whose wife's mother was at the very end of her life the mainstay of the family, came to grief over a difference with a bull walrus the very next spring. So, for every reason, the subject as well as the practice was wisely avoided. But he felt that a large, hearty devil might well lick his lips over such fare.

"Atokwok told me that he had put his hand through this thing." Peeguk's voice was stubborn, but his bowels felt as though they were turned to water.

"I do not know or care what Atokwok said, but it is true that he, being admitted to that place for a short time, came out very quickly with his face the colour of sand when it is mixed with mud where the white foxes play at the edge of the water. Also he did not ask to go back, though the chief of the fort was willing, but took his kayack and started for the anchorage of the whaler that brought him."

Peeguk glanced apprehensively at the ship from which he had just disembarked, then his jaw stiffened. Had he not come a matter of twenty days' journey to see this thing? He felt in the leg of his long walrus-hide boot, and brought out a sheathed skinning-knife with a bone handle, a twelve-inch blade and an edge like a razor. Testing this reflectively with a leathery thumb, he gave a little grunt.

"I go to seek this devil," he said curtly, and, turning uphill, strode toward the fort.

To the man behind the counter—there was much profitable trading done here—the request was made known, the brown face a mask for feelings many and mingled. It then appeared from what he was told that the thing had been brought by a medicine man six moons ago as a present for the chief of the fort, that no such devil had ever been seen in the North before, that it came out only in the dark, and that though it was a white man's devil an exception could be made for himself since he had come so far.

"Then it cannot get loose?"

"Only when the light shines in the dark, and then when it is permitted."

"Atokwok told me it went across to the wall on a bridge of light."

"That is what happens."

"And otherwise it lives in a box?"

The trader nodded. A patient man, used to dealing gravely with those who were only aware of first principles, he could enter into the mind of this hunter with the quick, black, questioning eyes and the soul of a child. The seal of the North was over them both. There were also mysteries on Peeguk's side, strange stories handed down from father to son of a Thing that walked by night, and, passing near an igloo, was shortly and inevitably followed by another visitor, even more grim and relentless. It had been heard and seen, but the full story was locked in pagan breasts where it would lie concealed. And there were other cardinal and more earthly mysteries pertaining to birds, animals and fishes that the short, brown people read at sight but no white man could ever decipher. Besides all this there was that which one feels for another if that other comes of a breed that will walk up to the hungry she-bear when she issues gaunt and ravening from her winter fast with her cub lurching beside her, and, taunting the great brute in his queer, clicking tongue, will drive his spear into her vast furry body. So, take it all in all, the trader found nothing to laugh at when he looked at Peeguk.

"There is much that is hard to put into words concerning this matter, but come you here after I have eaten, and you shall see for yourself."

Peeguk went out, and for the next three hours sat on a rock not five yards from the door. His stomach was empty but he craved no food. At times he took out the knife, tested the edge of it with his tongue, and put it thoughtfully back. The feel of it was good against his leg. At nine o'clock, when it was as dark as it would be for the next three months, the door opened.

"Come, and fear nothing. While this thing is on the wall it is not permitted to any man to speak. You may laugh or cry, but no words."

Peeguk took a look round before he went in. The grey of the Arctic sea tilting flatly up to the horizon—rock ledges, worn smooth by glaciers in the distant past—the low island buildings, hugging the solid earth as though they feared being uprooted by winter blasts—a cluster of topecks just above tide level—a few hungry, mangy dogs—the miniature whaler, riding, slack-chained, in the bay—and, over it all, the suggestion of illimitable space and emptiness. This was very familiar. Now it was in his mind that he might never see it again, for all that the trader said, because the trader did not know what he proposed to do. But he only made a soft little noise in his throat, and followed. And this, perhaps, was the bravest thing he ever did in his life.

The room, the biggest in Fort Herschell, was used indiscriminately as a church when a missionary came that way; or a court, as it had been when a magistrate journeyed five thousand miles to try Tetamagama and Alikomiak concerning the murders for which they were subsequently hanged; or for trading when the rush was on in the springtime. Some of the whaler's crew sat on benches at one end, with a few other whites. Behind them was a small wooden house with a hole in one side. Peeguk noted that this hole was of the size of the nose of a jar seal.

"It is the devil-house!" he whispered to himself, and took the seat nearest the door.

Someone turned out the lamp, and a moment later light was visible inside this house. A voice spoke, saying that all was ready. Peeguk did not stir a muscle, but the hair crawled up the back of his neck.

Then out of the hole in the devil-house leaped a great light that hit the opposite wall so that there came a space like a very white cloud and very round. At the same time was heard a sound like small gravel running down the bank of a stream, or many, many rifles being cocked quickly one after the other. In the white cloud appeared something Peeguk did not understand, but knew to be the writing of white men; then a face, very large, the face of a woman who opened her mouth showing many teeth, and smiled at him—Peeguk, the husband of Oomgah. At this his soul quivered within him, and he was glad Oomgah had not come. After that another white woman, also beautiful, and with as many strong teeth, but not fat enough for a good wife. Then two men, evidently not hunters, because their necks were thin and their shoulders narrow. They also looked at him and went away, and behold, the white cloud remained without a mark. Of a truth this was great magic!

His brain began to reel, while, mutely, he searched his past life for something by which he could judge this matter. There was not anything. He desired greatly to get clear of this, but was mysteriously anchored to his seat, not frightened as much as he expected, but reduced to helplessness because there was so much beyond his understanding. When one has travelled four hundred miles, one wants to understand. It would be no use trying to describe this thing to Oomgah. It would pester him for the rest of his days.

He became aware that these spirits, for they could be nothing else, had something to do with each other. One man and woman rubbed noses. He understood that. The other man saw it, and was angered. This also was comprehensible. There were many devil things they got into and out of, black like porpoises, things that ran about over the ground and carried people in their entrails. Peeguk did not worry about this end of it, because he expected that the males were going to fight about the woman. He had seen several fights about women in the last few years. So now he tried to soothe his palpitating heart, and waited. Also he loosened the knife that lay against his right calf.

It came before he was ready for it. One man—or devil—sat smoking, the woman having melted away from him, when the other came up very quickly from behind and stabbed him between the shoulders. Peeguk did not think much of the stabbing, because he who did it evidently knew little about the proper use of a knife, also when a man was stabbed he generally twisted about on the ground for a while before he died, whereas this one died at once. But great anger stirred in the pagan breast when, a little later, the murderer came upon the woman and, taking her in his arms, rubbed noses very hard indeed. She did not like it, and fought with him.

Peeguk writhed on his seat, hot fury mounting in him. He had seen much the same thing before when Ugnuk carried off Pilyuka, the Cross-eyed One, and wife of Tolpan. Tolpan had stabbed very efficiently when he caught them. But here was a woman who had none to help her. She went on fighting, her hair flying loose like much dry seaweed. Then, just as she became all soft, and bent like a fish in the arms of the murderer, Peeguk, who had suffered all he could, saw red. Whipping out the skinning-knife, he rushed across and drove it deep into the man's heart.

In that instant several things happened. There was a great shout that filled the room as with laughter; the murderer faded away as a salmon swims under the ice; the gravel-like noise ceased altogether—and there was the knife sticking into the breast of the woman! At that the stomach of Peeguk stood upside-down within him. He gave one loud cry and fled for the open air.

Oomgah, the Moon-faced One, had come at her leisure to the mouth of the Mother of Rivers, paddling close to the shore while the dogs yelped and scrambled westward over the barren land. The journey was nothing to her. She fished, trapped, slept as much as she liked, and in a general way enjoyed a sort of rest cure. As to Peeguk she had no anxiety. He might come at the end of two moons, but if it were three, what matter? She rather expected him to do some visiting first.

She was therefore surprised when, a week ahead of time, she saw his kayack floating like a dry leaf opposite the camp. He came ashore, rubbed her nose in a rather thoughtful manner, asked a few ordinary questions, ate heartily, and resumed life in the good old-fashioned way. But never a word he said of what had transpired at Herschell Island. She endured this for some days, then went at him.

"It is in my mind that after talking with Atokwok you journeyed to see certain magic. Did you see it?"

He nodded stolidly.

"It was great magic?"

"Too great for a woman to understand."

She turned that over for a moment, and presently sent him a knowing glance.

"Where is your skinning-knife with the walrus-tusk handle? Mine is broken."

"I lost it, and therefore bought another. Also I bought this for you."

He drew out a small packet, the contents of which had cost him much thought. It was a purchase made from the cook of the whaler on the way back from Herschell Island, and paid for with an otter skin. He had anticipated awkward questions from his life's partner, questions he was not prepared to meet, so with the wisdom that may be found on the Beaufort Sea as well as off it, pitched on the oblique method of evasion. Women, if diverted, give no trouble. Therefore divert them. He handed Oomgah the packet.

Inside she found a four-inch shaving-glass, backed with copper. Her lips widened in delight as she stared into it and saw the moonlike, globular face, with rows of rusty teeth, broken and jagged from much chewing of walrus hide. Here was a great treasure, and what a husband was hers! So she laid her round oily cheek against his, gurgling her satisfaction.

"It may be that you saw other women at the island?" she said throatily.

He shuddered a little. "Yes, one devil woman."

"Was she beautiful?"

He made a gesture, and surveyed her critically. "Yes, but not so beautiful as you."

"Then she will not come between us?"

"Never!" said Peeguk triumphantly. "I killed her!"

THE PASSING OF CHANTIE, THE CURLEW

THIS is a tale of the year of the great sickness that came to the small brown people who live on the shores of Grant Island where it fringes the eastern borders of the Beaufort Sea. Of necessity such tales are told simply, as one speaks to a child or to those who are very old, for they deal with those who walk carefully and are slow of speech. And the reason is that death is never very far away.

The North is a stern mother to the tribes that tenant her silent places. She feeds them for a time, then, perchance, starves them. She bakes them under a torrid sun and, in a little while, strikes them with killing winds. She smiles across leagues of sunny waters that soon are hidden beneath endless fields of grinding ice. She dangles her purple Aurora in the zenith that all may see and marvel, but out of her unknown regions come roaring the storms that no man may face and live. So beneath her threats and caresses the brown people are what they are: brave, simple and uncomplaining; wistful, because they know not when the end may come; loving the slant-eyed children for whose safety they are ready to die; generous, because hunger is brother to all, and, when old age comes, facing the final great adventure with unquestioning fortitude and faith.

Chantie, the Curlew, was smitten with many years. The last great event in her life had been when Oulibut, the Shining Ice, went the way of his fathers in a fine new igloo with a walrus tusk on top to signify that this was the place of death. She never forgot that, even though life had gone hard with her ever since. Now she was sixty-five. The way she reckoned this was by the number of times she could remember the breaking up of the ice on Beaufort Sea added to her age when she could begin to count. And at sixty-five she lived with Metauk, her son, and his two children, Tilligoo and Nanook. Metauk had married late, and soon after the children came his wife had run a poisoned fish-hook into her palm and gone out into the unknown, babbling strange and non-understandable things.

It was the year after that when the great sickness came to Grant Island. Elsewhere it would have been called measles, and treated accordingly, but to the small brown people it was a scourge laid on them by the Great Spirit who had a habit of expressing himself in various recognisable ways. One could, therefore, but wait and see how heavily the punishment would fall. So the scourge spread from point to point, from bay to bay, from igloo to igloo, till morning after morning there set forth fewer and fewer hunters over the field ice, and in the scattered igloos the tribe of Metauk lay on their backs with swollen and distorted faces, staring at the curving walls that shut out Unorri, the North Wind, indifferent alike to the yelping of famished dogs and the dwindling complaint of starving children.

They died—here a hunter, there a woman and there a child, and what became of the dead it were better not to ask. Perhaps the white foxes knew, or those lean and dreadful shapes that came by night from the nearby hills. Simultaneously it seemed that the salmon deserted the shallow waters, for they swam no longer with slowly-waving fins beneath the igloo's floor, while the sinew line with its bone hook hung slack and motionless in the emerald depths.

And if within the homes of the tribe of Metauk there was disease and death, the surrounding plains held that which was equally forbidding. Day after day, night after night, droned Unorri from the speechless north, unconquerably bitter. With the wind came a fine driving snow that stung like hot sand and made even the polar bear blink his yellow eyes. The outlines of the rocky ridges were smoothed into gentle curves; the stars, when visible, were diamond pin-points immeasurably distant; across the ice-fields vast pressure ridges were thrust up, creaking and groaning, and even the ancient earth herself seemed to contract and shrink beneath her spotless blanket.

It was the finger of Fate that kept old Chantie from the curse. It may be that she was too dry and shrivelled to yield to disease. Her gums were fleshless, her skin like parchment—brown and crackling with age, and her eyes had receded till they were no more than black slits in a leathern mask. Her chief sensations were love for Nanook and Tilligoo, and a consciousness of having forgotten many things. She was famished like the rest, but her hunger soon became submerged in a vast pity for the children. At night she lay awake for hours, pinching her withered breast and thinking of the days when Metauk's small sleek head lay against her warm smooth shoulder. She wondered if Oulibut, who had gone to the place where there was always good hunting and fishing—and no sickness, could see them now, and what he thought about it. Just then the children stopped babbling, and she became aware of a voice thick, and scarcely recognisable. It was the voice of Metauk. He had turned on his side so that she could just make out his distorted face.

"How long have I been thus?"

"I know not, but for many days."

"Then give me food. My belly is like a water-hole in which there is no water."

The old woman shook her tousled head. "Were there food Tilligoo had eaten it long ago. There is none."

At that Metauk propped himself up. He was not a pretty sight, for his head seemed as large as his body.

"Then go to the igloo of Aivick and ask for seal meat. All women are fools, especially the old ones."

"There is no meat in that igloo," said Chantie patiently, "nor will Aivick bring home any more. The sickness took him and he is dead."

Metauk made a choking little noise in his throat. "Speak then to Pituluk or some of the others, for the walls of my stomach are cleaving together and the strength has run out of my bones."

"Pituluk is even like yourself, calling for food when there is none to give. The salmon have gone down to the floor of the sea, and the curse lies so heavy that there is not one hunter who can take up his spear. The white foxes are fat, but the tribe of Metauk is very lean."

"And the sickness has spared you, O! worthless one?"

Chantie nodded. She knew that she was worthless. About all that she had been good for during past years was to chew the edges of walrus skins to make them soft for sewing into boots and kayack coverings, which meant that her teeth had dwindled to a few jagged roots. The sickness had doubtless spared her because she was not worth the taking. It was not any sign of humility to admit this. The thing was obvious.

"What is there I can do?" she croaked despondently. "The Great Spirit walks about in the storm and is angered. Who am I to reason with him?" There is no blood in my body, or I would give it to the children; and I, too, am very weak."

The hunter groaned and lay back. Fire was in his veins and strange lights danced before his eyes. There was no strength in him either. Further than that, he was filled with a queer sense of shame at his own impotence. It cut him to the heart that his children should be famished and he unable to feed them. Why should he be struck down, and this old crone spared?

"Do what no other woman has done in the tribe," he grunted sarcastically, feeling the fever overtake him again, "and go out and kill something that we may eat."

Chantie did not answer. Presently she stooped

over Nanook and put the end of a strip of walrus hide between the boy's dry lips, at which they began to mumble vigorously. It was all there was to suck in that igloo. Her mind was working slowly, and creaked while it worked. She did not fear death for herself, but did not want to leave these small ones to die alone. Outside came a whimper from the dogs. Days ago she had tried to spear one of them, but the team had danced away out of reach, reading only too well the meaning of the weapon that quivered in her skinny hand. By now they themselves were half-mad with hunger, and, reflected Chantie, dog would soon eat dog.

She drifted off into a sort of blind wonder at what it all meant. She could not remember having deliberately offended the Great Spirit, but something must have happened. Through her pagan mind passed the simple panorama of pagan life. Killing and eating, sleep and journey, effort and rest, the igloo in the lee of the pressure ridge, the straining sledge wriggling between a multitude of hummocks, the square flipper, warm and bloody beside his air-hole, the writhing salmon on the igloo floor, life and death and dim memories of affection in olden days, the passing of Oulibut as passes a chief—these were the pictures on the screen of her mind. She was thankful for them. They almost warmed her.

It was hours later when there came suddenly from the team a new note in which fear and excitement were sharply mingled. Metauk heard it through his stupor and began to babble of the hunts of other days. Chantie heard it, and the blood in her ancient veins coursed the faster, for with the voice of the dogs was a deeper, hoarser sound, half-cough, half-grunt, that was unmistakable. The white bear walked abroad that night.

She waited, and the sound came closer. The monarch of the North was in no danger from Metauk's team, and he seemed to know it. A half-starved dog meant no more to him than a snowflake. It was plain that he too was hungry, for there was anger in his grunt and his shuffling stride was carrying him nearer and nearer to the rounded dome of the house of Metauk. He could not catch a dog, but there was quarry here for the taking. Presently he upreared his gigantic height, took one vicious stroke at the nearest dog that broke its back, and laid his broad, sharp-taloned paws on the curving walls.

Chantie trembled and shook the hunter by the shoulder.

"Awake, Metauk, and kill," she quavered, "or you will die in your sleep, and all of us with you."

But Metauk could not hear, having drifted off to regions where even the white bear was harmless. He only mumbled unintelligible things, pushing out his swollen lips and tossing his fevered body. Tilligoo and Nanook as well were unconscious, a shapeless, tumbled mound in the half-light. The terror of Chantie rose to madness and she wrung her withered hands. The claws of the bear were cutting deep grooves in the rounded roof. Presently he would get foothold and climb up. Then the roof would collapse.

At this moment the querulous complaint of Metauk came back to her, demanding why she did not go out and kill something that he might eat. She had wondered vaguely what there was that an old woman might kill, and now, impelled by a strange impulse, she reached convulsively for the hunter's long, stiff-bladed spear. She shivered at the touch of it, for this meant death, but there seemed nothing else to do. And the bear's paws were just two feet from her grey head, with the snow wall between. She did not look at Metauk or the small motionless figures on the sleeping-ledge. It was time for an offering, and just one way in which to make it.

Crawling out on hands and knees, she looked up and saw a white pyramid, at the base of which snapped the surviving dogs. Never before had she beheld such a bear. There was a glimmer of moonlight in which his fur took on a sheen as of silk that rippled in quick waves with the play of his deep shoulders. He stood like a giant of a man, his lean arrow-shaped head turned savagely at the pestering team, his long black claws distended, his massive forearms reaching nearly to the centre of the igloo dome. At his flanks danced the dogs, weak with hunger, jaws open, nostrils wrinkled, staggering as they attacked, their yellow bodies fired with an ancient enmity. It was a battle of the strong against the weak, to which there could be but one end.

As Chantie crept into view the brute dropped to all-fours, recognising a new and different opponent. The man smell came to him, and he stood, swaying with a slow rocking motion, while instinct moved disturbingly in the sleek skull. Then the old woman heard a roaring in her ears that came from her own pounding heart, and made one weak, uncertain thrust.

It was only a pin-prick and drew no blood, but it roused in the beast the inherent timidity of man which lurks in all animals, great and small, so instead of one swift stroke of the broad paw that would have crushed out whatever life remained in Chantie's withered body, the lord of the North lunged at the frenzied dogs and began to shuffle toward the distant hills. Simultaneously the old woman, who by this time had cast away all fear, perceived that with him would go all prospect of food. And it was for food that she had made ready to die.

It must be that in times of utter stress humanity is able to discard all human weakness and clothe itself with prodigious if transitory powers. In such periods the vital flame achieves an unwonted brilliance before it flickers into darkness, and mortality scales hitherto unconquered heights. So it was with Chantie, the Curlew. The knowledge that those few who were left to her, and whom she loved with all her pagan soul, were sick and starving, and that their salvation depended on the oblation of her own worn-out body, was all-sufficient. The strength of youth flowed back in a swift, penultimate tide, bringing with it a strange fire that crept through vein and sinew and revived wild memories of days long past. Her fingers stiffened over the spear, and she stood upright, straighter than she had stood since the day when Oulibut went into the igloo with the walrus tusk on top. She was not old any more. Her voice came back, displacing the raven-like croak of later years, and with that voice, vibrant and contemptuous, she addressed the dwindling figure of the lord of the North:

"Are you then a rat and the son of many rats that you run from a curlew? Do your knees knock together while you seek shelter with your wife who hides under the snow that she may bear you a son in peace? Your hide is thick but your blood is thin, and your heart like that of the small cross-beaked birds that come when the sun is warm. Stop, therefore, that I may pull your heart out and give it to the dogs."

Now whether it was the dogs that snapped at his heels or the effect of this stream of derision poured out by the ancient crone as she stumbled gasping through the drifts, no man can say, but something penetrated the great carcass so that the bear halted, and, turning, upreared himself, as though to put an end to so outrageous a situation. Chantie, seeing this, realised that her race was nearly run, and what there was left for her to do must be done very quickly. Therefore she crept up as close as she dared, and, dropping on one knee, wedged the butt of Metauk's spear into a cranny of projecting ice, sloping the weapon forward so that it pointed directly at the great white chest.

"Come, O! coward with the spirit of a fish," she quavered shrilly, "and I will throw your entrails to the dogs."

The white pyramid swayed forward to bring this pigmy assailant within reach of the thick forearms.

Chantie involuntarily shut her eyes, for the lean head was now directly above her own. Then amid the furious barking of the team she heard a choking grunt. The spear shaft quivered and bent. She could see nothing, the world being blotted out by the huge overhanging body, but her stiffened arm grew suddenly wet. For an instant thus while the vast weight seemed to poise above her, till, with a crack, the shaft splintered in her grip, she felt something stinging and searing bite into her side. Then the heavens fell and crushed her into the snow. The last thing she heard was a muffled barking that sounded as though it came from a long way off.

She struggled back to consciousness a little later, feeling that her side was on fire and her face buried in fur, close and choking, making it hard to breathe. Slowly her eyes cleared. She was partly under the bear, which was lying still with the dogs guzzling at his rent flanks, while the double-edged spear projected stiffly from the prone carcass. Chantie had no feeling of triumph, but only of extreme weakness. The fire and the frenzy had passed, leaving her an old, old woman, wounded to the death, and with her final offering yet unmade. There was little time now in which to make it.

She managed to twist herself free, and with ultimate effort dislodged the spear. The dogs took no notice of her, being too busy stuffing their empty bellies with hot meat. The spear she found was but a poor cutting instrument, and it took precious moments to hack off a lump of dripping flesh. Even as she toiled at this the strength ran out of her like water, and her stiff fingers became caked with a grisly glaze. Then the snow fell again like a ghostly blanket in which she pitted her dwindling vitality against the onslaught of storm and bitter cold. She did not think at all, but only laboured, her lips set tight, a strange flicker in her glassy eyes. And with every movement it was as though the spear were penetrating her own tortured side. The final oblation was nearly made now.

Ten minutes later, Metauk, who was lying motionless in his skin sleeping-bag, felt something familiar touch his mouth. He could not open his lips because they were too swollen, but every fibre in his famished body thrilled to the taste of fresh meat. There was no asking whence it came, nor could Tilligoo or Nanook put the question, but all three lay and sucked in strength from the wild body that so late had roamed the frigid spaces of the North. The life of the white bear was now theirs, and flowed mysteriously through every vein. Their faltering heart-beats steadied, their chilled limbs grew warmer, till presently sleep crept in through the igloo door and spread its beneficent cloak over the home of Metauk the hunter.

But there was one whom sleep did not reach. Chantie sat silent in the gloom, waiting for the sands of life to run out. She managed to light the stone lamp by using a little of the bear's fat, and laid the rest of the meat close by the faces of the sick ones so that by no chance could they miss it. She pulled in the sinew fishing-line and rebaited the bone hook. If a salmon came now he would not pass that. She arranged the broken spear with its stained blade by

Metauk's side, that her son might not accuse her of carelessness, for good spears were scarce on Beaufort Sea. Then because her breast was burning so that it hurt horribly even to breathe, she pulled the hood of her walrus-skin tunic over her head, and lay down on the floor with her face against the igloo wall. There was nothing more she could remember to do.

Hours passed. Unorri, the North Wind, ceased to moan, and over the whole stark wilderness spread a strange calm. The stars came out and with them a quivering Aurora that shook its gleaming banners in the zenith and shed a soft radiance over the home of Metauk. The satiated dogs curled up and slept, while four gaunt forms stole down from the hills toward the stiffened body of the white bear. All else was motionless, breathless and empty, a vast and stinging void above which the springing dome of diamonded sky rose with a great encircling sweep.

It was nearly morning before Metauk moved. He felt better—and not nearly so hungry. His lids opened more freely. Turning, his mouth touched meat. It was frozen solid, but what difference! He began to tear at it, driving in his strong teeth with ever-increasing energy. Presently he stopped eating and puckered his copper-coloured brows.

"Is it then Pituluk who has killed the bear that I dreamed was climbing on the roof of the igloo, or," and here the hunter chuckled derisively, "is it perhaps that an aged curlew with no feathers in her tail has gone out and brought me the heart of the lord of the North?"

But Chantie, the Curlew, did not answer.

THE AFFAIR OF KALAUK, THE SKILFUL HUNTER

IF you journey by way of the Fox Channel and Boothia Gulf, turning north along the edge of the Beaufort Sea, you will come to the place where Kalauk, known to his friends as the Skilful Hunter, sat in the lee of a wind-whipped rock and stared thoughtfully at the Arctic Ocean. At a little distance, Kinniuk, the Orphan, played industriously with the bleached skulls of five square flipper seals. For the rest of it there was an apology for a tent, made of walrus hide, Kalauk's skin-covered kayack, lifted delicately beyond the reach of the waves, a spear or two, three lean and scabious dogs, a battered, up-ended sledge—and that was about all—except the Arctic Ocean.

But Kalauk was not conscious of anything being missing—for nothing was missing. All his stock-in-trade was here, everything by which he and the Orphan survived and wrested subsistence from land and sea and ice. He wondered sometimes how Kinniuk would fare if he were cast on his own resources, because the boy seemed interested in all but hunting and fishing, which was a serious handicap for an Eskimo youth. Also at the moment Kalauk was racking his wits to contrive how he would get along that coming winter with three dogs instead of four. Now the way the fourth had gone was by virtue of a disagreement with a polar bear whose hide was by this time in Dundee, being carried thither by the whaling captain who happened along just as the row was over. Presently the father of Kinniuk made a little noise in his throat whereat the dogs glanced at him suspiciously out of the tail of their narrow eyes, for this was summer time in which all the dogs of the North are doubly treacherous.

"We shall go to-morrow," he said briefly.

The Orphan balanced one shining skull on the other till he had built up a grinning pyramid. "And where shall we go?"

"Anywhere the seal and salmon are to be found. I shall take the kayack, while you and the dogs take the shore."

"And the tent?" put in Kinniuk anxiously.

"If the weather be fine I shall take the tent also, but if not it shall be yours to carry. Have I not said this same thing to you many times already?"

Kinniuk only grunted. As a matter of fact he had heard this edict pronounced ever since he could remember. He also knew that nothing was quite so hard to bear, and nothing made him quite so furious as to go stumbling over rocks and hills for endless miles with that shapeless lump balanced on his shoulders and watch at the same time his father skimming along a mile from shore with only an occasional stroke of his long double-bladed paddle.

Then there were the dogs. He confessed privately to an aversion for dogs, which in itself was an extraordinary thing for an Eskimo of any age. And it seemed now that he spent most of his life with them—which was perfectly true, because there was no other society whatever. The real trouble with Kinniuk was that he felt unutterably lonely—and did not know it. His mother had died years before when the woman's oomiak, or skin boat, had capsized in a bay of Ellesmere Island while they moved camp in the absence of the hunters; and since her Urnak, or guardian spirit, had appeared several times to her husband, with warnings of what would happen if he took another spouse, it was very unlikely that the latter would take any chances whatever in this intimate business.

"How far do we go this time?" said the boy sulkily.

"Till you reach the spot where I shall be waiting for you," was the placid answer.

Kalauk did not say anything more, but chewed contentedly at the last fragment of the last square flipper seal he had killed. There were more where that one had come from, so he did not worry, and even should he not kill for the next few days, he was fat enough and oily enough to exist for a considerable time without serious discomfort. What he really wanted was another dog. And there were no females left in his team after that incident with the polar bear the winter before.

About noon on the following day Kinniuk flung

himself down on a ledge that overhung a long narrow bay, and fixed his black eyes on his father's kayack that danced lightly from wave to wave something more than a mile distant. He had never seen anything quite so effortless in his life, though he had seen it many times before. The boy himself was exceedingly hot from the awkward weight on the small of his back, and the dogs seemed possessed of many devils. The naked country all round was shimmering in the bright sun of the short Arctic summer, and except in the lee of the ridges there was no shade. He dared not leave the bundle of walrus skin for an instant, or the dogs would have got at it. Presently the nearest of them put a long quivering nose into the air, sniffed at something that crept into his black, expanded nostrils and sent out a quick, excited whimper. In the next moment he tore off straight inland, his lean belly close to the ground, and the other two leaping after him so closely that they looked like a narrow, dirty wave of yellow fur. Kinniuk blinked. He could not swear. And this for the reason that only those folk who claim to have escaped from savagery know how to swear.

From a spur of the stark hills that lifted to the southward came a wild medley of sound, in which the frenzied barking of Kalauk's team was punctuated by another note, higher, sharper and even more wild. Kinniuk held his breath and listened, till there shot into his mind a startling thought that made him forget instantly about the bundle that was torturing his soul. And at that he dashed off, rolling as he went like a coal barge in a gale, for the Eskimo is built for strength rather than speed. In ten minutes he knew what the trouble was.

Squatting on its haunches in the midst of the pack was a thing which save for the length of its legs was half the size of the smallest dog, and Kinniuk knew it in a minute for a wolf pup. It was not the brown wolf of the timber country far to the south, nor yet the wolf of the Land of Little Sticks, but the great grey Arctic wolf, the terror of the North. The dogs seemed to know it too, for even now when it was but a quarter grown and had but a fraction of its ultimate strength, they danced just out of reach of the long jaws and sharp teeth that were already formidable. But Kinniuk saw that the odds were too heavy and the end could not be far away. The grey flanks were already torn, and a gaping cut widened in the bony shoulder.

And then a curious thing happened, for the wolf's eyes met the boy's eyes and it seemed that in some strange way there flashed from the former a sort of swift, proud appeal. Of course, as Kinniuk instantly realised, it could be nothing of the kind, but nevertheless there sped between these two pups of the North, animal and human, that which was in some mysterious fashion mutually understood. Simultaneously, and this was strangest of all, every vestige of fear was emptied out of Kinniuk's heart just as one empties sea-water out of a skin bucket. He saw the wolf pup—and loved it. He saw the yelping dogs—and for the first time in his life despised them.

Now it is given to some to understand, and to others to seek diligently and yet understand not at all, and this applies to both men and beasts. So if you ask how it was that Kinniuk was able to cast away all fear, and how it came that the wolf pup, when the boy had beaten back the snarling team, lurched weakly forward and with an upward glance of narrow, yellow eyes laid his lean head between the boy's feet, it may simply be said that the North has mysteries of its own, and the empty spaces of the world are not more devoid of wonders than the teeming city.

Thus it came that in the fullness of time the team of Kalauk, the Skilful Hunter, was made complete, but it is told along the shore of Ellesmere Island and in many a cranny of the Arctic that in the making there was much tribulation. Between Amerauk, the wolf, and the dogs there was warfare till the increasing strength of the former, combined with the sharpness of his teeth and his amazing quickness of action, brought him gradually but surely to the leadership of the team. Through battle after battle he forged steadily ahead, and with scarred flanks and long white cicatrices on his bony skull emerged the undisputed master. Kalauk stood by, marvelling, and held his peace, for it seemed that with the wolf pup the boy Kinniuk was also finding himself. It was after watching wolf pup and man pup hunt the coast caribou that Kalauk consulted Kitamauk, the Sorcerer, who happened to come that way, and was told that the matter was none of his affair. Then, not being entirely satisfied with Kitamauk, whose reputation in the Beaufort Sea was somewhat questionable, he broached the subject direct on an evening when he was full of seal meat and good-nature.

"How is it, Kinniuk, that you, being once afraid of dogs, have now no fear of a wolf? It is not many months since your courage was like the sea-water that runs away through the sand till there is nothing left."

The boy grinned contentedly. He was curled up in a shapeless mound, his fingers playing with the long white hair that waved on Amerauk's throat. The lank jaws were open, disclosing a red cavern of mouth, roofed with black. The brute lay motionless, his yellow eyes fixed on his master.

"We understand, the wolf and I—that is all."

"But it is not written that a wolf can understand, unless he be possessed of an evil spirit."

Kinniuk shook his head. "His spirit is not evil. I think it is that of my mother which has returned. Then why should I fear it?"

Kalauk glanced at him sharply. If here indeed were the spirit of his late wife, there was nothing for him to fear either. His mind went back to the time when Chiooka, which means the Woman with the Round Nose, was alive, and it began to appear that he had not always treated her quite as well as he might. In fact he distinctly remembered several occasions when he had not. So it seemed uncomfortably possible that Chiooka, who had been very devoted to Kinniuk, was seizing this opportunity to return to earth and even the score. Kalauk had been about to venture stroking the beast, but this last reflection made him hesitate. Just then Amerauk yawned, and one could see about a foot farther down his throat. The hunter decided not to do any stroking at that moment, and Kinniuk made a little gesture of amusement.

"It is in my stomach to ask you why it is that you are afraid of the wolf if I am not, especially should this be indeed your wife." The boy drawled this out in a voice that Kalauk found distinctly irritating. "Would my father, who is known to be brave, not do what I do?"

"Thou art a fool. All my life I have done that which would turn thy bones to water."

"Look," said Kinniuk, and, rolling over, took the brute by one torn ear, then, with a chuckle, thrust an oily hand straight into the cavernous mouth. Amerauk did not stir, but a quick light dawned in the savage eyes and the saliva dripped from his rigid jaws. For a moment thus, man pup and wolf pup, till with a little laugh the boy withdrew his slimy fingers and gave that terrible head a playful push as though to signal that the game was over.

"Will my father, the Skilful Hunter, do this? Surely *his* bones, which are more ancient than mine, will not turn to water."

Kalauk hesitated, feeling as uncomfortable as he had the summer before when a bull walrus decided to come to the surface immediately beneath his kayack, with results that were nearly disastrous. Also he noted that Amerauk was now regarding him with an expression remarkably like the one which used to rest on the face of Chiooka when he had been more than usually unkind. It suggested that the time was coming, and it puzzled him greatly to imagine just how a wolf could manage to convey that idea. So, putting all things together, he could see no reason for taking any chances that might be avoided.

"It may be that thy mother, being regretful at having given birth to so great a fool as thou art, is now sorry for thee and will not bite," he said contemptuously: "and, because she had thee for a son, is now punished and made to wear the skin of a wolf. Of these things I will speak to Kitamauk, the Sorcerer, when he returns this way from his hunting."

A low growl rumbled threateningly in the shaggy throat, at which Kalauk moved a little farther off, while Kinniuk laughed delightedly. "My mother says that it will be well for both you and Kitamauk if there be no more talk of this matter." He got up, shook himself and laid a caressing hand on the lean head. "Now we go to hunt the coast caribou, Amerauk and I, for it seems that the hunting of my father is of no avail and we be hungry, we two together." He paused, then added meaningly, "If Amerauk should run perchance on thy spear when the night is dark and be killed, the spirit of my mother may take on another shape which would please thee even less than this one. It is well to think sometimes of these things, and to-night there will be much meat."

He strolled off, the grey shape at his heels, while Kalauk stared silently after him. The conversation had taken a most unfortunate turn. It was perfectly true that the Skilful Hunter had contemplated putting a sudden end to these embarrassing circumstances, but he had never imagined the possible results as Kinniuk now pictured them, and no man could look forward to spending the rest of his life in trying to kill his late wife every time she assumed a new guise. The whole affair was full of awkward complications, and the more he reflected the more puzzled he got. Just then the hunting cry of the grey wolf sounded from inland, and he ran quickly to the top of the nearest ridge to watch Amerauk in action.

Lying on his stomach, he peered eastward over the great tundra, which now in the swimming warmth of summer was a series of long, low, rolling undulations of rock, covered partly with tufted moss and interspersed by lakes where the wildfowl reared their families with a whistling and calling and quacking that went on day and night. Between two of these lakes he discerned a small band of coast caribou, all females who had come north without the bulls to bear their young. There were perhaps a dozen of them, crowded close together, the calves in the middle and protected for the moment by the jostling of their mothers' tawny yellow bodies on which the new hair grew in great smooth patches, for this was the season when fur and feather in the North discard their old coats ere donning the new ones that nature so marvellously provides against the bitter weather to come. But Kalauk was not interested in this, which was an old story to him. His eyes were fixed on a lean, yellow-white shape that darted in dizzy circles around the terrified deer.

It seemed that Amerauk was playing with his quarry ere he struck. Faster and faster he flew, his shaggy belly close to the ground, while the terrible head, thrust straight out in dreadful expectation, and the white brush trailing straight behind, transformed him into a sort of arrow of destruction. He moved not as a dog moves in leaps, but in a sort of streaming rapidity that was independent of time or distance, an animal projectile, sharp of tooth and of inexpressible ferocity. Kalauk waited and held his breath. What chance had anything that lived in the North, save only the white bear himself, against an enemy like this?

Presently Amerauk wearied of his sport, and, swerving like lightning, made one vicious upward stroke at the throat of a trembling cow whose body projected a little farther than the others. Kalauk's eye, sharp though it was, could hardly follow, but he noted in the next moment that the cow had begun to stagger, while from the frightened calves came a piteous bleating. The group swayed, lost formation, recovered it again and huddled still closer. The large soft eyes were fixed on the common foe, but there was nothing to fight with, and the sharp horns of the bulls were five hundred miles away in the Land of Little Sticks. Amerauk swerved again, and this time, as though in a royal and savage disgust at such helplessness, dashed straight in, fastened with one leap at the cow's throat and pulled her down. The band wavered and broke. Came a clatter of flying hoofs on the bare rock and the big beasts dispersed in winged terror, some to the east, some to the south. In a moment the wilderness swallowed them, calf and cow, till there was left only that half-dead mound of matted hide. with the gaunt brute fastened at the torn throat. And then, most terrible of all, there rose into the throbbing silence that note of fear which speaks of peril in the empty spaces, the grey wolf calling to the pack.

It was an hour later before Kinniuk, burdened as to the shoulders with a bloody load, tramped into camp. At his heels was Amerauk with bulging sides, and it was evident that man pup and wolf pup had both eaten to the full capacity of their stomachs. Kinniuk dropped his trophy at Kalauk's feet without a word, which the latter found particularly irritating, while Amerauk, with his black lips lifted a little, rejoined the team. The team smelled fresh meat, looked furtively at their leader, and did nothing. Kinniuk's skin was full to bursting, and for a while he said not a word, but lay on the flat of his back, his fat hands under his oily head.

"Where will my father hunt this winter?" he hazarded after a long silence, speaking casually as though it did not really matter very much.

"It is in my mind to go to the Bay of the Black Rock, there being shallow water at the mouth of the bay where the square flipper is found. But what has a child to do with such things?"

"Perhaps nothing, but it may be that the spirit of my mother will have something to say."

Kalauk felt a sudden surge of anger at this impertinence, and put out a hand as though to take the boy by the ear, when in that second something drew his eye to the leader of his team. The beast was staring at him with just the expression of resentment that Chiooka used to wear when he lost his temper in the years that were past. At least this is what Kalauk thought he recognised, while added to it was a warning rumble in the shaggy throat totally unlike any sound Chiooka had ever made. Hastily he withdrew the hand, wondering hotly whether in all the country there could be another Skilful Hunter in such a position as this.

"Where else would I go?" he replied, disregarding all reference to his late wife. "Besides, there be many wolves in the hills behind that bay and it may be that Amerauk would like the company of his kind."

Kalauk threw out this last in a sort of bravado, when, in a flash, the great idea came to him. Other wolves! The more the better, for their desolate cry would drift into his camp night after night with its ghastly invitation to the leader of his team to come out and hunt and kill, till after a while Amerauk would vanish like a spirit indeed and be no more seen. And after that he would be well content with only three dogs. The more he thought of this the more he liked it.

"Are you answered, O! wise one?" he concluded sarcastically.

Kinniuk nodded. "We are content, Amerauk and I."

Now this was the way of it, and in the days when fur and feather made ready for the bitter weather, the former by putting on their winter garments and the latter by winnowing their marvellous flight thousands of miles to the south, and when the lakes and pools were stiff and glazed and snow had begun to gather in the hollows of the naked land, Kalauk made camp in the Bay of the Black Rock and spent much of the night listening for those wild voices which would surely come before long from the dark hills in the east. Duly in the small hours of a dead still morning they did come, faint but unmistakable, and instantly drifted back the answer of Amerauk with a wild and savage fervour that made the blood run cold.

"It will not be long now," whispered the Skilful Hunter to himself, and rolled over and slept.

Thus began a strange season in which Kalauk knew not whether he was dealing with dog or wolf or devil. When morning broke, the brute was always there, but often it was plain that he had filled his belly meantime. No man saw his comings and goings. He was still leader of the team. He did not shirk his work, and pulled with the best of them. But if the days were Kalauk's, the nights were his own.

Kinniuk would sometimes say that he had heard Amerauk hunting the night before, then take the great head between his knees and stare curiously into the formidable eyes. By degrees Kalauk learned not to notice things, but was conscious of being watched with a ceaseless vigilance. The situation had begun to burden him heavily, when one day there grew a dark speck far out on the field ice and an hour later Kitamauk, the Sorcerer, drove his panting team into camp. Kalauk breathed a sigh of relief when he saw who it was, and, as Kinniuk happened to be out with Amerauk, the Skilful Hunter at once opened his heart to the wisest man on the Beaufort Sea. Kitamauk, chewing stolidly, listened unmoved, save only for an occasional flash of his small black eyes. He had known Chiooka. Presently he gulped down a final fragment of raw and frozen seal meat.

"It is written that the spirit of any man or woman may return to earth, having first chosen the shape it will take, but of many such happenings this is the most strange."

"Have I not said it is strange?" replied Kalauk impatiently.

"That is true, but you have not seen that the strangeness is because Chiooka, having once been a woman, now takes the form of a male wolf."

Kalauk started. "I had not thought of that."

"There can be but one reason, which is that while she was a woman she was so unhappy that she has refused longer to be a female of any kind."

"But if indeed she does not like me, why then does she stay and pull my sledge?"

"It is not for you, foolish one, but for Kinniuk that she stays. Also there may be that she has forgotten, and returns thus to perform it."

Kalauk felt more than ever uncomfortable, and put a greasy hand on the other man's knee.

"Then you, wise one, shall tell me what I must do, for there is not anything I would not do to put an end to this since it makes a sickness in my stomach. Nor is there anything I will not give thee, even to the knife I have from the captain of the whaling ship and the carved tusk that Cunayou, the Image Maker, gave to Chiooka many moons ago. Speak, therefore, because I hear the voice of Amerauk in the wind, and like the wind he comes quickly."

Kitamauk seemed undisturbed. "A thought rises in my mind as the square flipper to his air hole," he said composedly. "Is there not left any of the bark of the red willow that you traded with the Yellowknife Indian who fished on Dead Walrus Island?"

The Skilful Hunter choked a little. There was some left, but he had not thought it worth while mentioning.

"It may be that half of the bag remains, and it shall be thine if the thought in thy mind keep on till it gets to the surface. What is this thought?"

Kitamauk shook his head, and just then Kinniuk shuffled into camp with Amerauk at his heels. He stared at the Sorcerer, saying not a word, but the wolf extended a sharp black nose that wrinkled suspiciously, then made a deep sound in his hairy throat. Kitamauk stood rigid till the tenseness of the moment passed, when Kimmiuk gave a laugh, and, at a gesture, the beast disappeared. The Sorcerer glanced after it, a wrinkled smile spreading on his aged face.

"I would smoke now," he said briefly.

He left next morning, divulging nothing further before he struck off over the field ice save that he would shortly return for the knife, the tusk and the tobacco. And with this Kalauk was perforce content.

A week passed in the Bay of the Black Rock and it seemed to the Skilful Hunter that the leader of his team was becoming more human at every nightfall. When the team was needed, Amerauk was in his place without a word of command. Out on the ice, the long whip-thong never touched him, because he never needed it, also because Kalauk had qualms about flogging the spirit of his late wife. So tractable was the beast, that he wished that Chiooka had displayed more of the same engaging qualities before she departed. As to the other dogs, Amerauk lorded it over them with a sort of royal disdain. They stirred not till he had selected the lump of seal meat he desired, then slunk forward, tails between their legs. Thus peace reigned in camp so long as dogs and man attended strictly to their own business. But always the brute was watching. Kalauk dreamed of him when he slept, and the belief grew in his mind that Amerauk was waiting, waiting for that which was yet to come. As for Kinniuk, the boy only grinned. He was happier than ever before in his life.

On the afternoon of the seventh day another speck appeared on the hard horizon, and presently Kitamauk's team scrambled over the rough shore ice. The Sorcerer ran alongside, while a shapeless lump balanced on the lurching vehicle. Kalauk stared till the lump detached itself and waddled toward his igloo. Then he saw that it was a woman. Instinctively he glanced over his shoulder, as he often did now, at Amerauk. The beast was erect, legs stiff, lips lifted and the long hair on his spine standing up like the back fin of a spring salmon. But, which was most amazing of all, the woman only laughed.

Kitamauk motioned her into the igloo, and with Kalauk crawled in after her. When they were seated, he coughed importantly and spoke thus:

"It is without question that the spirit of Chiooka inhabits the body of the wolf that follows thy son, and being that of a woman is therefore more troublesome to deal with. So it came to me that the only way was to call upon another woman, who is the more likely to understand, we being but men, you and I. Thus it is that I have brought my sister, Kasiaga, the Flat Face, for whom I have not been able to find any use these many years."

Kalauk looked at him in wonder. The face of Kasiaga was undoubtedly as flat as an ice pan. Also her teeth were nearly gone, the few remaining ones being worn and broken from the interminable chewing of much walrus hide. Her skin was like old brown leather, and as tough as a whip-lash. What powers had such a one, marvelled Kalauk, to charm away the spirit of Chiooka? He could understand her brother not finding any use for her. Then Kitamauk's dry tones came in again:

"It is written that while a woman, or even the spirit of a woman, will stand much from a man, she will not stand anything at all from another woman. Why this is I do not know, but it always has been thus since the world began, whereof the place is not far from here. Also, since I myself am tired of the Flat Face, I bring her to thee for a wife, and if after this thou art troubled further with the wolf Amerauk, you need not give me the knife and the tusk and the bag of Yellowknife tobacco. I have spoken."

Kasiaga croaked like an amused raven, but Kalauk gasped. He did not want to marry again, especially a thing like this. And what would Kinniuk say? He pushed out his lips, tried to speak, floundered, then made an ineffectual gesture.

"It has come to me in a dream," continued the Sorcerer suavely, "that you should be very thankful. Otherwise Amerauk will without doubt demand soon that by right he shall sleep in thy igloo beside thy son. Furthermore, if thou attempt to kill, the spirit of Chiooka may inhabit next the body of a white bear."

Silence fell beneath the icy dome, and Kasiaga looked more ugly every minute. But she would not be as difficult to handle as a jealous wolf. Kalauk had to admit that. He was still wavering when Kinniuk pushed in on hands and knees, glanced sharply at Flat Face, and turned to his father.

"Who is this woman, and where is Amerauk?"

The Skilful Hunter drew a long breath. "The woman is thy new mother, and where Amerauk is I know not nor care."

Nor did anyone know, even the Sorcerer himself. Amerauk had vanished like a cloud in the night, taking his terrible but defeated way back to the silent places where he joined a pack that hunted in the hills of Grant Island and along the shores of the Beaufort Sea. In a week he was the leader of the pack, killing the old grey bitch that had governed it for months past. And often in the season of bitter weather that followed, Kalauk, as he journeyed homeward spear in hand, was shadowed by a great, gaunt form that watched him with fierce, resentful eyes as it drifted like a lost spirit from rock to rock.

THE SALVING OF PYACK

It fell on a night in the bitter season of the year that Peeguk, the Flat-footed One, was heavy of heart. Unorri, the North Wind, had been pressing down out of Boothia Gulf for weeks past with a weight so heavy that it could be felt through the twelve-inch walls of his igloo, and now he stared moodily at his second wife, Oomgah, the Moon-faced One, a grim question in his black eyes. She sat huddled on the snow bench, holding close a shapeless bundle. The bundle was Pyack, the Late Comer, now nine months old. Pyack had arrived in the spring of last year with the grey geese from the south.

The heart of Peeguk ached in many places. The stone lamp was fed by a shred of seal fat, and when that was consumed there would follow a great darkness. It was hard to be hungry in the dark. One would also be cold. So there were three enemies to be faced at once. The reason it would be cold was that when the fires of the body run low for lack of fuel, there are opened mysterious passages by which the enemy of frost may enter. And he always does. They both knew this.

For many days the North had been shrinking, flattening and cowering beneath the onslaught of Unorri. Ridges were smoothed out and crowned by long, crystalline folds from which was whipped constantly a fine, dry rain of powdery snow, paralleling the earth six feet deep, a stinging, driving punishment that the lord of the North himself did not care to face. No food was afoot, no track of pad or claw imprinted that vast and chilling blanket, so that even the grey wolf ravened unfed. And when he starves there be many furred bellies that go empty.

Peeguk, in the past month, had worked inland from Boothia Gulf, much farther inland than he had ever been before. This because the ice had jammed thick and solid against the coast, vomiting up great pressure ridges thirty feet high, so that the air holes of the jar seal were almost impossible to find, and for the first time in Peeguk's life the ocean had ceased to be his larder. That, and the weight of the unending storm, drove him south in search of caribou. He had saved a little seal fat for Pyack and the stone lamp.

It seemed that there were no caribou. Day after day he scourged his dogs over the empty plain, and night after night saw them staggering back unsatisfied. Their ribs projected like barrel hoops, their flanks were dry sinew, their pads were cracked and bleeding, the pointed ears lay flat on the lean skulls and the bony shoulders thrust loose into their walrus-hide collars. One morning he found four dogs instead of five, and a week later only three. Now three dogs cannot pull a sledge with a woman and child and the family gear—even three that are not famishing. This fact moved poignantly in Peeguk's mind as he stared at his wife.

"I will kill one," he said, after an hour's silence.

She held the Late Comer a little closer. Without dogs a man cannot travel. In the North he who travels not, starves—with those who be with him. On the other hand, there was no milk in her breast now—but only love, and Pyack could not be fed on love. Were this possible, he would be fat—very fat. What frightened her was the alternative with which they were faced.

"Can we not wait another day?"

"The dogs will not wait. Never before have I known one dog to eat another. It is a very great hunger."

The Late Comer gave a weak whimper, and she felt the small lips pucker, questingly, against her side.

"Ey-yah, my husband! And what then?"

He fingered his useless spear. "It may be the storm will be over. Till then the white foxes devour each other in their caves, and nothing stirs."

He crawled out next morning and grimly surveyed his dogs, half-buried in the snow. Their narrow eyes never left him. Which, he pondered, should he kill? Not the black-eared bitch that led the team. The other two were younger. With bitterness in his heart he approached the nearest, but the starved brute caught the murder in his glance and leaped away. He flung his spear and—missed! He, Peeguk, missed!

The fact sobered him. Too late to do anything more, for all three were circling warily, just out of range, as wise as he, and as loving of their hardbitten life. Dog against man, it would be now, and what end might not come to this! The long hair bristled on the lean backs, and, his heart growing cold within him, he turned and crawled in toward Oomgah.

"The dogs—they know. I tried to kill one, and missed. They are now our enemies. I go to hunt again, so you will stay here. Do not come out."

He stooped over her and, very gently, touched the hidden head of the Late Comer. Oomgah did not speak, but looked steadfastly into his eyes. It was all there, the fidelity and tragedy of the life they had shared together. She wished that Pyack had not arrived—it hurt her so when he cried. But evidently they were all about to die together, and Pyack had only been hungry—really hungry—for three days. The skin was drawn tight, like brown parchment, over Peeguk's face, his voice was hollow, and she knew that the strength which had been her pride and safety had run out of his back and arms and legs. It might be that he would not return to the igloo, but die in the open, in which case the dogs—or the wolves would find him. If he did not come back she could only seal up the entrance with a block of snow, cover her face—and wait. So, because she was aware of all this, and knew that he also was aware, she spoke no word, but only nodded. Then Peeguk stooped and went out.

He could never remember much about that day, except that the dogs were with him, keeping a hundred yards off, one behind, one on each side.

Or were they wolves? He was not quite sure, but they appeared through the snow flurries, moving like phantoms that gave no tongue. The wind did not seem so heavy. He had curious visions of square-flipper seals basking, of salmon crowding up to the shallow spawning grounds, half-feathered geese waddling near their nests, stranded whales, cow walrus, very sleek and fat, sunning themselves—and all this within a spear's length. But something told him they were not really there—only the dogs.

He did come back—though empty-handed; bent, snow-plastered, feet that dragged, his inward fires burning low, his visage a frosted mask through which the eyes of the man glowed, hot and desperate. Caribou were in the country! He had seen them, miles away, drifting, a ghostly herd, across the horizon with life, heat and salvation in their round and jostling bodies. He followed for a while, hoping that the wolves might pull one down, or one go lame. But none went lame, and the grey wolf hunted elsewhere. The dogs came back with him, squatting round the igloo, watching, waiting. Now that they feared each other, they kept the same distance apart. Peeguk knew what they waited for. But that, he vowed, would never be.

It was then that there came a rift in the wind. The stinging drive went out of the powdery snow. It settled, leaving the air clear. The drone of four weeks past softened to a whisper and died. The seared feeling in his eyes lessened, and he saw a great white star burning in the south. In the same moment the old bitch put her black muzzle into the still air, sought out and captured some indefinite signal that reached her from the beyond, cocked her pointed ears, and began a tremulous whimper that swelled and consolidated into a long, long howl. The other two joined in.

The heart of Peeguk leaped within him, but he dared not stir. The dogs were looking south—where the star was. That meant other dogs, other life! Then, with a shriek, the wind began again, the powdery snow was once more driven like dust, the star vanished, and he was left sucking the ice block that covered his short bristly moustache. He stooped, saw the snow plug at the entrance, kicked it away, and felt inside in the dark for Oomgah. He put his arm round her shoulders.

"Come—we start now. There is a camp not far to the south."

"It is too late. My legs have turned to water, and I cannot walk."

"You need not walk. Put Pyack close to your heart and sit on the sledge."

"You have the dogs again?"

"I am many dogs to-night. Come!"

They lurched southward, wallowing through, she a squat pyramid of snow, he a staggering but indomitable figure, one with the storm itself, equalling its ferocity in the strength of one ultimate purpose, squaring his shoulders that the wind might aid him the more, his bones like aching rods, sinews like burning wires, the heart of him pumping defiantly, his whole tortured, striving frame calling up its last ounce of strength and resistance. Something lay to the south, how far he did not know, yet something. The dogs had gone for it, but their trail was instantly obliterated. At times the star gleamed through, so he followed that, Oomgah swaying behind him with that which was dearer than life held close to her dry bosom, concentrating on this one beloved morsel all the warmth in her fainting body.

She did not know how long it lasted, but the sledge never stopped once. It seemed like hours after they started that she saw a gleam. It was the roofs of a cluster of tents, with high snow walls and lights inside. Then a great barking of dogs, and voices. She knew that Peeguk tried to lift her from the sledge, but fell in the snow and did not move.

The rest of it was a dream. When Oomgah woke she felt warm and comfortable, with the Late Comer sleeping next her side. She lay very still, examining the tent with half-lidded eyes, soothed by a tide of strength that crept reassuringly through her body. No sound of wind now. Peeguk stretched on his back close by, his eyes shut, his face blistered with frost patches. Near Peeguk sat a white man who looked at them not at all, but made a writing in something that she knew was a book. She wondered how he got the writing to put there. At the back of the tent was a small iron stove, and she recognised the odour of flaming oil, a different kind of oil. A lantern hung from the ridge-pole, this pole being the biggest piece of wood she had ever seen except when the whaler came ashore on Lost Island. There were piles of robes, and boxes. The white man had a red face, red hands, a short brown beard, and his eyes were grey like the sea when the snow comes and the black swans fly south.

Another man came in, looked at the strangers, and handed the first one certain small things covered with snow. These being observed very closely, more writing was made in the book. Then the man said something and went out. Soon after that the red-faced one stood beside Oomgah.

"You are better now?" He spoke in the Husky tongue, a little stiffly, but quite understandable.

She nodded.

"Your name?"

"Oomgah." She touched her breast. "There is also Pyack, of nine months."

He smiled. "I have seen Pyack. And this man?"

"Peeguk, my husband."

"You have come far?"

Oomgah did not know. "Two moons ago we left the ice because there was no food. What place is this?"

Macgregor's tawny brows lifted a little. He had been sent out by the Government at Ottawa to make records of temperature and snowfall, and learn in general what might be learned of this section of the wind-whipped North. He saw these to be Coast Eskimo, and the spot where he now camped was three hundred miles from salt-water.

"It is not any place when I am gone. How did you find me?"

Peeguk, who had opened his eyes and was listening intently, made a sound in his throat.

"The bitch, who is leader of my team, smelled something when the wind dropped. Then the storm came again, covering the dogs' tracks, but there was a star, and I followed that."

"A star?" said Macgregor gravely.

"There was nothing else to follow."

Silence spread in the tent, and Peeguk said no more, it not being his place to do the talking. Oomgah sent him a look and touched her breast again. All was well with the Late Comer.

"And if there had been no star?"

Peeguk made a gesture. "I do not know. My strength had all run away."

He of the red face nodded understandingly. "You will eat now for the second time, only a little, for it is not well to fill an empty stomach too quickly."

"The second time?"

"Yes, the second time since last night."

Peeguk marvelled, yet held his peace. But he wanted greatly to know about the dogs. Presently he asked.

"Their bellies are full. We are camped by a lake, and there are many fish under the ice."

Macgregor disappeared, and a Yellowknife Indian brought food in bowls. Peeguk, like all Huskies, hated the Yellowknives, but this was no hour for hate. So he took the food from the slim brown fingers and closed his eyes, burdened with a great wonder. The inward fire of his body was glowing now.

In the morning he stood on his feet, a man again. The storm had roared itself out, and the high clear sky held not a cloud. A bright sun transformed the wilderness into an interminable fleece, deep sprinkled with captured constellations. Their myriads of diamond facets sent out a blinding brilliancy of refracted blue-white rays. Northward from camp stretched a nearly obliterated furrow that marked the tortuous passage of the sledge.

Macgregor, a quiet man, who had his own way of doing things, talked with Peeguk that day, saying that he needed a hunter, and the Yellowknives were of little use in those latitudes. The thing was settled with few words, and Peeguk told Oomgah as he punched his spear-handle in the snow to find a drift wind-packed to the right point for igloo building.

"It is very simple. I will have a rifle, better than the one I lost through the ice, and we will reach the sea when the geese come north."

"Perhaps it is well, but there was fear in my heart this morning."

"What kind of fear?"

"In the topeck the red-faced one opened a box. I saw many strange things small and black, as in a nest. These he fastened together at the top with fine iron sinews, very many of them. Then I saw four bottles, very small and standing up straight. There was light in those bottles, but no fire."

"You asked nothing of this?"

"No—it being in my mind that this was a devil-box."

Peeguk scratched his head, remembering the devil-woman who stuck to the wall at Herschell Island and could not be scraped off, and the man he had tried to stab, but who escaped leaving the woman with the knife in her breast. Many questions had moved him concerning this matter, but so far he had not found anyone who could answer.

"I will speak to the red-faced one," he said gravely, "and it may be this will do no harm. I have only known of two kinds: one that speaks with a voice, and thereupon makes a noise like a dog scratching the ice; and that other at the island, of which I told you. Keep silent, therefore, till I know more."

Oomgah kept very silent. Above all things, Pyack must not be exposed to any malign influence. She was very grateful to the red-faced one, and his eyes were kind, but to her all white men were mysterious. They had so many potent things at their command. So, when Peeguk finished the igloo, which he did very soon, slashing out the big curved blocks so that they fitted without any trimming, she crawled in thankfully, and felt much more at home. Peeguk, on the other hand, went straight to Macgregor.

"My woman says that you have a devil-box in the topeck. Is there danger to the child?"

Macgregor understood perfectly. "There is danger to none. It is a spirit-box, and not of devils."

Peeguk, knowing something about spirits, felt

happier. A spirit was the thing that went out of you when you died, went clean through the wall of your igloo, journeyed to find those of your family who had gone before, gave them the latest news, and lived with them thereafter in a place where there was much food and no wind.

"To-night," added Macgregor, "you shall hear it."

"Does it make a noise like a dog scratching the ice when its speech is done?"

"No, not that one. Not always can I hear it myself, and but seldom in storms. But to-night will be fine, and," here his voice softened and he looked oddly at Peeguk, "on this day it says that which is said on no other of all the year."

"How comes this voice?"

"Through waves of air," said the red-faced one as though to himself, "and over the clouds from far away." Then he laughed, while his eyes grew kinder than ever. "It travels like the eagle, but more swiftly. And to-night I think it will speak to you."

Peeguk immediately told all this to Oomgah, and she came out and sat in the sun and watched Macgregor. He had set up two poles, and joined their tops with a long piece of iron sinew. From this he led another bit into his topeck, where he remained busy for quite a time, till suddenly sounded such a strange noise that the old bitch, whose ribs now bulged as though she had swallowed the Late Comer, put her tail between her legs and howled grievously. The other dogs joined in, whereat Peeguk beat them to silence.

Now the rest of that day was like any other day, till, at nightfall, the red-faced one summoned all in camp to his topeck, leaving the door-flaps open. One could already see some stars, the biggest of them being that which Peeguk had followed. When all were seated, the Huskies farthest from the Yellowknives, Macgregor looked at his watch and, nodding, put his hand in the spirit-box. Peeguk saw the light born in four small bottles, and held his breath.

For a moment nothing. Only strange sounds and many clicks. Then, close beside them, the voice. High, clear, pure as crystal, a voice that sped on invisible wings. Over rigid lakes, rockbound coast, snow-buried forest, over the fields of ice and desolation unspeakable it came. Out of the heavens it descended, the voice of a child, penetrating the cabin of the trapper, the hidden trading-post, and wherever man might spread his intercepting filaments.

"And there were in the same country shepherds abiding in the field, keeping watch over their flocks by night."

Thus sang the voice, and sang on, telling of a star that men followed while the world was young. Peeguk and Oomgah did not understand a word except about the star. That was natural enough. Macgregor's eyes were fixed on these children of Time. They too had followed a star. There came to him the vision of a Woman on an ass, a Babe at her bosom, and it seemed that between that Woman and Oomgah, between the Judæan Child and the

Late Comer with his small, pinched, copper-coloured face and strands of coal-black hair, was every tie of kinship. And the arms of Mary, Mother of God, in which Divinity rested on a Galilean hillside, why did they differ from those of Oomgah behind whose dark, low-lidded gaze moved a thousand questions that would never be answered? So, thinking of all this, he did not notice that the others, reckoning the affair to be over, had slipped away, leaving only Peeguk and his family. Presently the hunter put out a venturesome hand and touched the box.

"It is very great magic. But may not this thing we have heard be also heard on some other day of the year?"

"On no other does it mean the same."

"Then it always comes in the bitter weather?"

"Always. Perhaps it is needed more then."

"Is it the day of the death of a great chief?"

"No," said Macgregor gently, "but of the birth of a Child."

Peeguk pulled down his black brows. "That is hard of understanding."

Oomgah looked at him. Then she drew the Late Comer closer to her breast, and began to sway with a slow rocking motion.

"Ey-yah, my husband," she murmured softly, "I can understand."